ho

many, many thanks.

Conversations with
AYCKBOURN

Alan Ayckbourn on the sands of Scarborough's south bay

Conversations with
AYCKBOURN

IAN WATSON

MACDONALD
MACDONALD FUTURA LIMITED
LONDON

MACDONALD
MACDONALD FUTURA PUBLISHERS
LONDON
Copyright © Ian Watson and Haydonning Ltd 1981

First published in 1981 in Great Britain by
Macdonald · London and Sydney

Macdonald Futura Publishers
Paulton House
8 Shepherdess Walk
London N1 7LW

ISBN 0 354 04649 7

Printed in Great Britain by
Purnell and Sons, Paulton

For all those who have made the Stephen Joseph Theatre such a special joy, particularly Ken and Margaret, Dorothy and Joan, and Stan and Doreen; for Alfred Bradley; and for Linda and Heather

CONTENTS

ACKNOWLEDGEMENTS

People in many parts of the world have helped in the preparation of this book. Sincere thanks go to them all, especially:

Mrs Acs and Mrs Nagy (Artisjus, Budapest); Leif Andersen (Jørgen Blaksted Teater-produktion, Copenhagen); Olga Andrić (Jugoslovenska Autorska Agencija, Belgrade); Alan Ayres (National Theatre, London); Bayerisches Staatsschauspiel, Munich; Ken Boden (Stephen Joseph Theatre in the Round, Scarborough); Peter Bridge; Peter Cheeseman (Victoria Theatre, Stoke-on-Trent); Sture Dufva (Svenska Riksteatern, Solna); Tom Erhardt (Margaret Ramsay Limited); Jean Gimonet (ATAC, Paris); Georges Goubert (Théâtre National de Chaillot, Paris); Michael Haensel (Theater am Kurfür-stendamm, Berlin); Malte Hartmann (Rowohlt Theater-Verlag, Reinbek); Ernst Hausknost; Zuzana Havlíková (Slovenská Literárna Agentúra, Bratislava); Sven Henning (Den Nationale Scene, Bergen); Dr Jiří Hlaváč (Dilia, Prague); Stig Jarl Jensen (Det Danske Teater, Copenhagen); Al Kalson; C. Kyprianos (Copyright Protection Society, Athens); David Land (Robert Stigwood Organisation); Philip Langner (Theatre Guild, New York); John Little (Australian Elizabethan Theatre Trust, Sydney); Bernard Martin (Victoria Theatre, Stoke-on-Trent); Elsebet Stanley Møller (Det Ny Teater, Copenhagen); Richard S. Morse; Yumi Nakanishi (Institute of Dramatic Arts, Tokyo); Olaf Nordgreen; John Offord; Margaret Ramsay; Tatemi Sakai (Orion Press, Tokyo); Henry-E. Simmon (Ernst-Deutsch-Theater, Hamburg); R H Smith (British Embassy, Moscow); Staatliche Schauspielbühnen, Berlin; Imogen Thomas; Sam Walters (Richmond Fringe Theatre); Stephen Wood (Stephen Joseph Theatre in the Round, Scarborough); and Kirsten Zagula (Gladsaxe Teater, Søborg).

In addition to digging out information and photographs, and checking drafts, Heather Stoney has sustained the project with several memorable meals; and Richard Johnson and Carol O'Brien of Macdonald Futura, have been unfailingly enthusiastic and supportive throughout. To them, special thanks.

11

INTRODUCTION

The only time I ever met Tom Stoppard was one Saturday afternoon when we found ourselves playing for the same cricket team. The closest I came to Harold Pinter was at a private supper party, when I played first slip to an intense discussion of cricket between him and Gawn Grainger.

Tracing a finger over Alan Ayckbourn's wall-chart planner, to find moments in the year when the conversations in this book could take place, I tripped over small, red, cricket ball symbols. 'Scarborough Cricket Festival', he explained, in a tone which strongly suggested that these dates were to be regarded as sacred. It would seem, *prima facie*, that there is somewhere a thesis to be written on the correlation between the obsessive game of cricket and modern British dramaturgy. This is not it. Nevertheless, it is that same Scarborough Cricket Festival which is responsible for this book, for it was there that I annually spent my youthful summer holidays, watching the lighter moments of Trueman, Hutton, Wardle, Benaud, Lindwall and Miller by day, and the early stirrings of James Saunders, David Campton and Alan Ayckbourn by night.

Scarborough is a solidly middle-class town which stands on the coast of north-east Yorkshire high above two very beautiful bays, separated by a crumbled, but still picturesque, castle. Everything there combines to make it an ideal place not to have a permanent company theatre. Its population of less than 50,000 is roughly half that which administrators reckon is required to sustain such a theatre. Its economy, based firmly in tourism, is seasonal and inevitably fluctuates with the climate. Its hinterland, the north Yorkshire moors and the Vale of York, is highly attractive and visitable; but the resident population is more likely to fetch up slaughtered and roasted on the dinner table, than alive and responsive in a theatre auditorium. Schools there are, and a college, but the nearest university is more than forty miles away in the City of York, which has its own repertory theatre.

It was in Scarborough, nevertheless, that Stephen Joseph found the right mix of circumstances and individuals to base a revolution in British theatre that was precisely contemporaneous with the revolution which George Devine was fostering with his stable of writers in Sloane Square. While Joseph, like Devine, was running a writers' theatre, it was on theatre form rather than the subject-matter of plays that his revolution was based.

In retrospect, the cause of theatre in the round might appear a limited one on which to base a revolution. Indeed, at the time, the journal of the young theatre turks who regarded the Royal Court as their Mecca – the much lamented *Encore* (incidentally edited by a man who worked with Stephen Joseph's company, the late Clive Goodwin) – while broadly acknowledging Joseph's work as bringing much-needed new perspectives into a dangerously moribund theatre, tended to regard his obsession with theatre form as, at best, a little irrelevant. For them, social content was all. The theatre establishment was more virulent: to a man, it embraced the new-found phobias of that prophet of Devine's revolution, Kenneth Tynan, concerning the rear view of actors and the uncomfortable proximity of their perspiration. Even when the establishment succumbed to Joseph's unfailingly charming rationalism and enthusiasm, it dismissed his passion for opening out the proscenium arch as sheer battiness. With the benefit of hindsight, it is impossible not to note that he was personally responsible for founding two of Britain's most exciting theatres – those in Scarborough and Stoke-on-Trent – and that, without his influence, many other theatres, including the National Theatre on London's South Bank, would, at best, have been far less stimulating structures.

About Stephen Joseph's influence on playwrights it is inevitably more difficult to give chapter and verse. He helped, fostered, tutored and gave opportunity to a great many. After the initial failure of *The Birthday Party*, he picked up and encouraged Harold Pinter. He guided and worked with David Campton, James Saunders, Mike Stott and the American playwright Michael Weller. And, of course, he drew out the mammoth writing talent of a teenage actor in his Scarborough company, Alan Ayckbourn.

Stephen Joseph's theatre in Scarborough was not the first theatre I had ever seen, but it was the first to give me ambition. Stephen, ever available to his audience, recognised and encouraged that ambition, and I became a student of his in the Drama Department at Manchester University. I first worked for him at Stoke-on-Trent in the traumatic period when, during his final illness, he was warring with another of his protegés whom he had appointed Director there, the excellent Peter Cheeseman.

From Stoke, I moved to Scarborough, in the closing months of Stephen's life, and it was there that I worked with Alan Ayckbourn. *Relatively Speaking* was already a big West End hit (despite my own review for BBC North Region radio which pooh-poohed it in terms which, I thought, would endear me to *Encore* and place me in line for Tynan's job on *The Observer*). *The Silver Collection* was to be Ayckbourn's great follow-up hit, and I was pleased to be its stage director. At the read-through, *The Silver Collection* (already advertised throughout the town) turned up as *The Sparrow*, and was denied an Arts Council New Play guarantee on the grounds that it would undoubtedly be very successful and make its author a lot of money. (Then, as now, the Arts Council was never so endearing as when it was hopelessly wrong.)

The Sparrow called for a setting of unbelievable grottiness. With my stage management team, I offered token disarray. 'Watson's a bloody useless stage manager!' shouted Ayckbourn. (Dame Edith Evans gave me a similar accolade some years later in Accrington, when, already well into her eighties, she undertook a tour of one-night stands for me in north-east Lancashire towns, and I, noting her to be in real danger of collapse from exhaustion, brought the curtain down before her encore.) Working on *The Sparrow*, I got my first inkling of what Ayckbourn means when he talks of 'playing the truth'. He had written filth, and filth he wanted.

Alan Ayckbourn has never been the writer that others have wanted him to be. He is temperamentally incapable of standing still long enough for critics to pigeon-hole him: perhaps this is why, almost uniquely among modern playwrights, he has still not been the subject of extended critical evaluation in a book. London critics have awarded him gongs for plays which audiences have steered clear of, and audiences have at times flocked to see plays about which the critics have been, at best, lukewarm, even grudging. The fact remains that, translated into twenty-four languages and constantly played throughout the world, he is our most successful living playwright; a paradox in itself, when it is recalled that he rarely spends more than two weeks a year writing. In Scarborough, audiences wait excitedly to see what he is going to offer them next: they respond to his unpredictability, and, after more than twenty years, they know that, whatever it is that he puts before them, it will challenge and probably delight them. No wonder he wants to stay there.

ALAN AYCKBOURN:
a chronology

1939: Born, Hampstead, 12 April.

1951: School at Haileybury.

1956: Left school. First professional theatre job with Donald Wolfit at the Edinburgh Festival.

1957: Joined Stephen Joseph's Theatre in the Round company at Scarborough.

1959: First and second plays, *The Square Cat* and *Love After All*, performed at Scarborough.

1960: *Dad's Tale* performed at Scarborough. National Service at RAF Cardington, Bedfordshire (2 days).

1961: *Standing Room Only* performed at Scarborough.

1962: Founder member (and Associate Director) of the company at the Victoria Theatre, Stoke-on-Trent. *Xmas v. Mastermind* performed at Stoke-on-Trent.

1963: *Mr. Whatnot* performed at Stoke-on-Trent (London Production: 1964).

1964: Left the Stoke company. Last appearance as an actor in William Gibson's *Two for the Seesaw* with Heather Stoney in Rotherham. Joined the BBC in Leeds as a radio drama producer.

1965: *Meet My Father* performed at Scarborough (London production, under the new title *Relatively Speaking*: 1967. Television production by BBC: 1969).

1967: *The Sparrow* performed at Scarborough.

1969: *How The Other Half Loves* performed at Scarborough (London production: 1970). *Ernie's Incredible Illucinations* published and performed in London. *Countdown* performed (as part of *Mixed Doubles*) in London.

1970: Left the BBC and became Director of Productions at the Library Theatre in the Round, Scarborough. *The Story So Far* performed at Scarborough (subsequently revised, 1972, as *Me Times Me Times Me*; London production, under the new title *Family Circles*: 1978).

1971: *Time and Time Again* performed at Scarborough (London production: 1972. Television production by ATV: 1976).

1972: *Absurd Person Singular* performed at Scarborough (London production: 1973).

1973: *The Norman Conquests* performed at Scarborough (London production: 1974. Television production by Thames TV: 1977). *Evening Standard* Best Comedy Award for *Absurd Person Singular*.

1974: *Absent Friends* performed at Scarborough (London production: 1975). *Evening Standard* Best Play Award for *The Norman Conquests*. *Plays and Players* Best Play Award for *The Norman Conquests*. Variety Club of Great Britain Playwright of the Year for *Absurd Person Singular* and *The Norman Conquests*. *Confusions* performed at Scarborough (London production 1976). *Service Not Included* (television play) transmitted on BBC2.

1975: *Jeeves* (with music by Andrew Lloyd Webber) performed in London. *Bedroom Farce* performed at Scarborough (London production: 1977. Television production by Granada TV: 1980).

1976: *Just Between Ourselves* performed at Scarborough (London production: 1977. Television production by Yorkshire TV: 1978). The Scarborough company moved from its seasonal fit-up in the library to its own year-round permanent theatre (subsequently named The Stephen Joseph Theatre in the Round) in a converted school.

1977: *Ten Times Table* performed at Scarborough (London production: 1978). *Evening Standard* Best Play Award for *Just Between Ourselves*.

1978: *Joking Apart* performed at Scarborough (London production: 1979). *Men On Women On Men* (late night revue with music by Paul Todd) performed at Scarborough.

1979: *Sisterly Feelings* performed at Scarborough (London production: 1980). *Taking Steps* performed at Scarborough (London production: 1980).

1980: *Suburban Strains* (with music by Paul Todd) performed at Scarborough (revived for London season: 1981). *First Course* (lunchtime revue with music by Paul Todd) performed at Scarborough. *Second Helping* (lunchtime revue with music by Paul Todd) performed at Scarborough. *Season's Greetings* performed at Scarborough and transferred for limited London season.

EARLY DAYS

IW   Your father was leader of the London Symphony Orchestra; your mother was a journalist; and you had a step-father, from the age of seven or eight, who was a bank manager. Which of those three exerted most influence on you?

AA   It must be my mother, simply because I was with her much more than with anyone else. My real father had a sort of romantic influence on me, in that, because he wasn't around, I tended to idolise him rather.

IW   So you didn't get taken to concerts?

AA   Not a lot. My mother took me a bit. She took me, for instance, to Brighton to meet Herbert Menzies, the conductor there; and I saw a rehearsal, I remember that very clearly. And she took me to the odd concert. But even if my father had been there, I doubt if he'd have taken me to concerts. Like a lot of professional musicians, he loathed music. He liked certain artists – he would listen to Kreisler, and thought he was wonderful – but he'd lunge across the room to turn off Beethoven's Fifth. 'Bloody old bore!' he'd cry. And I suppose, if you're sitting sawing it out day after day under Beecham and such people, that's not what you want to hear when you get home. But he liked light music: I know he always loved Al Bowlly and all those people. And I do remember him listening to certain pianists – Rubinstein and people – and enjoying them.
    I listened to radio a lot and then later I had a gramophone and I spent a lot of my early money on records – all classical stuff. That was my first influence, not pop at all. I never bought pop.

IW   Your father wasn't around after the age of about five?

AA   Not really. He married again and went to live in Norfolk. He gave up music. To all intents and purposes, I don't remember him being at home. We moved to Staines, Middlesex, I remember – that was where I had my first schooling, when I was about the age of four – and he wasn't there then. He used to pop home occasionally.

IW   Your mother was a journalist. What sort of journalist?

AA   Well, I think journalist is the wrong description. She wrote. She started as a novelist. She wrote several novels which were published by Michael Joseph. He encouraged her and she knew him well. When she got married, I suspect, her career dissipated a lot, and it was

Alan Ayckbourn at the seaside with his mother

only when my father went off, and times got hard again, that she had to start to support us. What she did become was queen of the short story world. She wrote – while I was between the ages of about four and fourteen, for ten years certainly – a phenomenal number of stories for magazines such as *Woman's Own, Home Notes, Woman,* which were syndicated; she was, of her type, a star. She worked in a very peculiar way; they used to send her illustrations and she used to write stories for them. And she used to tell of the peculiar code of each magazine: I can't remember exactly what, but in *Woman's Own,* at that time, (for example), your girl heroine could fall in love, but not with a married man; then in another magazine, you could have a married man, but they must have an unhappy ending. There were various codes. And she wove in and out of these codes, and somehow managed to write original stories.

IW   You sound as if you read them all.

AA   No, I didn't read them. I watched her write them, because she used to thump them out in the kitchen. And it sounds a corny anecdote, but she really did – I suppose if Mummy had been washing up all day, I'd probably have become a very good washer-up – she gave me a little typewriter and I started to thunder out my own awful tales. I wrote stories and *I* wanted to be a journalist: later things changed! When she married my step-father, she continued to remain quite independent. Having married the local bank manager, she decided she didn't want to stop writing; in fact she was in the supertax bracket for quite a long time. She earned more than he did. The marriage was quite a surprise to me. I was away at boarding school and she said: 'I'm getting married . . . '

IW   And you wrote her a letter: 'Dear Mummy, I hope you'll have a very happy marriage. Love, Alan.' Which is really a terribly desperate, sad little letter. Were you just not happy about the idea?

AA   It was supposed to be good wishes! I wasn't *very* happy.

IW   You had no brothers or sisters?

AA   I had a step-brother.

IW   So the bank manager had a son; was he at school with you?

AA   No, he never went to school with me. He was much, much younger. My step-father tended to take care of his education and my mother took care of mine. And they each said: 'Leave my kid alone.' That was the feeling. So my ma paid for all my education.

IW She sent you away at what age?

AA Seven. I went to the local boarding school. Actually, I came home every weekend. We were living in Billingshurst; and then they got married, and he was having a bungalow built, I remember, in Wisborough Green, so we moved in there. And we used to go for school walks past the bungalow and raise our caps to my mother.

IW Were you happy about being away at school?

AA I didn't mind going to school. I was very unhappy when I first went; but then I quite liked it, and I think as time went on I got on very well at school. I had very many mates, because a lot of local kids were there. I didn't get on *very* well with my step-father: I got on better with him when I was older than when I was younger.

IW The evidence of the plays you've written in your adulthood seems to suggest that the home that was provided by your step-father might have been a major formative influence, in terms of subject matter. Is that fair?

AA Well, yes. My mother had a very tempestuous relationship. They had a lot of rows. But you know, kids are marvellously adaptable: I mean, we weren't really upset, or marked.

IW Is there any element of exorcism involved in using this background in your plays? Are you trying to work it out of the system at all?

AA No, I don't think so. I remember at the time wondering why my mother had got married again. The horrible bit came much later – what happened to her. I cruised on; and what happens to you if you're a boarding school child, is that you get a tremendous detachment from your home, which, if the home is at all rocky, is not a bad idea. You come home and look at it, and you get angry about things occasionally, and you get upset; but you're not really touched, because it's not any more your base. What worried me was that I did see the relationship – from being away from it – deteriorating, which was a bit worry-ing. And later on, one day I came home and my mother looked awful, and there was talk of getting her shock therapy. Then came one of the few positive acts I've ever taken: I'd left school just . . .

IW So you were just seventeen at this time.

AA Yes, and she was still at home. I was just going to Edinburgh for the Festival, and I was in London rehearsing. I found her a flat, and a job as an assistant to some writer. He was some madman who threw books at her, but nevertheless he got her back working. She'd stopped writing, dried up; she'd got very unhappy.

IW   This was through the marital upset?

AA   Yes, it had all gone wrong.

IW   It sounds like curious shades of *Just Between Ourselves*.

AA   She was going Vera-like. It was extraordinary.

IW   Going catatonic.

AA   Yes, it was quite a worry. She took this job, and I said: 'I'm off to Edinburgh for three weeks.' When I came back she met me at the station. And she'd got jeans on! She was about twenty years younger. It was absolutely amazing – the best thing I ever did. I'm sure she'd be dead now if I hadn't done that.

IW   Some time before that, you went off to Haileybury. Presumably about eleven, was it?

AA   Twelve, actually. I was a bit young to go. I won a bank scholarship. Barclays Bank gave away quite a few – three or four – scholarships, mainly based upon scholastic achieve-ment at one's prep school, but also based, I think, eventually on interview in Lombard Street – whither I went, in my grey suit.

IW   You said earlier that you were tapping away on your toy typewriter while your mother was writing her bits for *Woman's Own* and so on. Were you consciously developing writing at this age or not? For school magazines, for example.

AA   I was very ill at my prep school, for a term. I don't think they ever found out what it was, but anyway I got better, so it can't have been that serious. But I adapted a Jennings book as a play, and it was done at the end of term. I'd got the acting bug while I was there: I'd played a Sea Scout in something, I remember – with glasses on, which I thought showed good character acting. And I then wrote this play, which they performed, though I never saw it. Anthony Buckeridge can now sue! I'd written myself in as Darbyshire, the character man, the part which got all the laughs. But I never even got to see it. That's my only writing memory. Oh, I'd written a story, one of those during-the-war spy stories – which I'd been told was rubbish, so I got a bit depressed. I was writing a bit of poetry. But I certainly wasn't playwriting – playwriting was third on the list until I got to public school.

IW   It was while you were at Haileybury, then, that you decided that the theatre was for you. How early did that come, and what did you see yourself doing in the theatre?

AA   Well, right up until the bloody last minute, I was still tinkering with a journalism career. But there was a master at school called Edgar Matthews, who had been a friend of Donald Wolfit's and, I think, at some point had organized tours for him as a production manager. He was getting near to retirement age and was teaching French at the school, and once a year he organized a Shakespeare tour during the school holidays, taking a party of boys off to the continent; to France and Germany and all over the place.

IW   In English, to the continent?

AA   Yes, schoolkids. He was a wizard of organization. He also directed the plays and his wife and daughters acted in them. You weren't allowed to go in for them the first year or two, but I auditioned when I was fifteen, I think; and I got into the first one I could. I got a small part, as Peter, in *Romeo and Juliet*. And off we went to Holland and we toured around there. And that was magic. That was the first real 'theatre' theatre I'd experienced, which was just terrific – you know, all that spirit gum and greasepaint.

IW   Who did you play to?

AA   Oh, quite a lot of people. I suppose they were the same audiences as Scarborough plays to now. A lot of people speak English in Holland. The English Speaking Union drummed up people. We played very odd places: some were quite good theatres, other places were quite primitive. I don't think our Shakespeare was earth-shattering, but it was fairly good.

IW   So you went in on this purely as an actor? You weren't in on technics at all; you weren't doing sound, lights, anything else?

AA   No, I was just acting. This was tremendous. And I think Edgar must have thought I had a bit of talent. The following year I came back, and he'd marked me down as a comedy actor. They were doing *Macbeth*, and I didn't want to play that boring old porter, so I plunged in hoping to play Macbeth. He really didn't think I was up to that – I didn't really have the weight, I was a six-stone weakling – but he did cast me as Macduff. And this was his swansong, this was the year Edgar was going to retire, so he decided to really go to town. He was going to take us round America. We went over on the *Queen Elizabeth* – the first, not the second – and we came back on the *Queen Mary*, and that in itself was worth all the money in the world: a group of public schoolboys, fifteen, sixteen, seventeen, getting themselves absolutely slewed all the way over – it was wonderful. And this was touring gone

Edgar Matthews (centre) returning from the USA with his Haileybury production of *Macbeth*.
(Alan Ayckbourn rear right, waving)

mad, because we had all the joy of touring with none of the professional responsibility. We didn't actually care if the show never went on. We arrived and we went up the east coast: we played in Maine, at the University there, and then we went up into Canada and played in Ottawa. And we played in Quebec, then we went down to Niagara and we played there; then we came through to Pittsburgh – it was a very strange tour, but we did see a hell of a lot of America by Greyhound coach. I don't think the whole thing was more than about two and a half weeks.

IW   The whole of Haileybury cannot have been theatre, though. Presumably, like most British public schools, it was fairly rugby-orientated, and sporty, and a whole lot of other, rather less salubrious, things. Did you take to it all right?

AA   It was tough to start with. My prep school had been an extraordinary place, because it had actually run down while I was there. The headmaster and mistress had decided they'd had enough of running this place for so long. So by the time I was leaving, there were only four of us left. It was idyllic, my last term. We'd passed our exams. So we stayed with this smashing couple, and we farmed and we looked after the place – they'd turned it into a farm. We fed the pigs and all that: terrific! So, going to Haileybury, suddenly, from that, where we were lords of the manor, we became, blup, right down there somewhere: it was a huge shock. And it was at the tail end of an era. You know, I read about it now, and they've introduced girls into the place: there seems to be some sort of semblance of equality. But it was still run, as most of those schools were, on the most extraordinary lines, where everything was done to make you feel unwelcome. It was a very tough school.

IW   How did you react to the public school system?

AA   Well, I think there's a way to do it and that's to play the system and create your own niche. And it sounds madly pretentious, but we formed a sort of bohemian section.

IW   We?

AA   Well, there were about three or four of us. This was two or three years in: it took that much time. Before that, you just hoped nobody noticed you. We behaved as we thought artists and writers did – you know, we didn't clean our studies much, and we were always a bit longer-haired than the others. We tended not to join in any of the functions, we were a bit anti-establishment, and we were thought of as a bit left. And people sort of gave us a wide quarter, including the masters. They used to rail at us a bit; we were by-passed for any sort of promotion – none of us ever became a prefect or was given any responsibility whatever. And, in fact, we joined in organized games. I wasn't too bad at cricket and I was an average rugby player, so we were in that side of it: we were out of the social and the more regimented side. And the school was big enough and flexible enough to allow that.

IW   Neither then nor, apparently, now – because both your sons went to public school – did you object to the system in principle. Is that right?

AA   It did give me a bloody good education. I don't say I took advantage of it. Everybody should be offered that: that's the answer to that.

IW   Just before we leave your public school education: you've done all this acting. Any writing?

AA   I used to write the house play at the end of every term. That was in the way of revue sketches, really. And I also edited the house magazine. Which, because I was such an inefficient editor and could never get any contributions, I used to finish up writing myself as well, under various assumed names. I used to type through the night on old stencils, and the housemaster used to stand over me furious, because his house magazine was always later than everybody else's. It was obviously a thing of great import in the staffroom. But no, I hadn't really started writing anything serious until after I left.

IW   You left at seventeen. There was never any suggestion of any form of further education, was there?

AA   They tried to persuade me, because I got the A levels I was asked to take – English and History – I was in the English Sixth. And they said: 'Well, you must go on for S level.' But honestly, by that time, I thought I didn't want to. Actually one was leaving because one didn't want to stay, rather than because one wanted to do anything. But, as I was leaving, I went to Edgar Matthews, the man who'd sent me off on tour, and said: 'I want to go into the theatre. Can you help me?' And he said: 'I have two contacts. One is Donald Wolfit, the other is an old boy of the school, Robert Flemyng. I'll give you letters of introduction to both. I don't know: I can do no more.' As it happened, Donald Wolfit was on the very point – I think the following Monday (I was leaving on a Friday) – of starting a revival of *The Strong Are Lonely*, a play he'd successfully had in London, I think, with Ernest Milton. He was reviving it with a slightly less starry cast – Robert Speight was in it – and was looking for someone to play a sentry, an acting ASM, really. Edgar had assured him, I think, on the phone, that I had been in the school cadet force and could stand at attention without fainting for forty-five minutes. So, in the most extraordinary way – and at that point Equity, as far as I knew, didn't exist – I joined his company and was rehearsing at the YMCA in Tottenham Court Road, with one or two lads straight out of drama school saying: 'Where did you train?' I said: 'Train?' I was tremendously green. I sat around the rehearsal room and did what I was told and gawped at all these – it was an all-male cast – these wonderful old actors.

IW   Yes, Wolfit has been terribly maligned since he died. There's the awful story which compares his Lear with Gielgud's Lear: Gielgud's was a tour de force and Wolfit's was forced to tour. Was he really awful?

AA   I had nothing to compare him with. He was awfully big! I'd never been that close to an actor of that size: I hadn't been close to any actor. And standing on quite a small stage and seeing this man towering through things, I mean on a scale that would be unheard of today –

IW   He was tall as well as broad, was he?

AA   He seemed very big. I don't think he could have been that tall, but he seemed enormous to me, in all directions. He used to wear cloaks and big black hats, and his hair was always brushed back; and there were his wonderful saturnine eyebrows, and this make-up line that was always in his hair, because it had been there since 1910. And everyone stood back and stood up when he came in, and he swept through. And his performances were majestic and huge; and they were all about acting, they weren't about anything to do with the character. By modern standards, it'd be quite a shock, I'm sure.

   I watched him very closely, because I was on stage. He'd fling himself on his knees at the end of the second act, after being excommunicated by the Pope's emissary. He began to kneel and say the Lord's Prayer, with tears rolling down his face – and he did genuinely move the audience. But as the curtain sank, he used to slowly turn his head upstage and just continue the prayer; but it became a vicious attack on the audience. 'Coughing bastards!' he'd say. And I was so shocked. I wasn't shocked by the blasphemy, I was shocked by the fact that a man could come out of such a moving moment with such apparent ease. And he could do that all the time. He'd fling lines upstage at you: 'Stand up!' he'd say, and carry on performing.

   We were playing in the Lauriston Hall, which is a Jesuit Hall, in Edinburgh. It was one of those exciting plays where you could start with the curtain open: it was an electric curtain. And, as I used to call the half, Donald would say: 'You know, there's no harm in a little drink before a show. Can you get me some drinks in here?' And he gave me some money. He said: 'I want a bottle of gin and six bottles of Guinness.' So I said: 'Yes.' He said: 'Don't let them be seen coming in, because you know what I'm dressing in, don't you? You know what this room is?' I said: 'No.' He said: 'It's the confessional.' I said: 'Ah, is it?' And he said: 'And the priests are outside, so can you bring them in quietly?' So I whipped out to the off-licence and I smuggled in these bottles, past these long-garbed, eagle-eyed gentlemen who were standing on the front step, smiling at the audience as they came in. And I took them to Donald Wolfit – and this is a true story that no one ever believes. He poured himself a gin, then he said: 'Some water.' There was no water, obviously, in his dressing room. And

I said: 'Well, the only water is at the other side of the stage, Mr. Wolfit, sir. And the curtain's up, so I can't get across.' He said: 'Use your initiative! There must be some water in the building!' And he strode away, with me in tow, crashed down this passage, opened the door, and we were in the chapel. And there was this barrel – I swear – that had 'Holy Water' on it. And he topped up his glass with holy water and said. 'You see what I mean?' I'd never seen a man drink gin and holy water before. Wonderful!

IW   He has a reputation for having surrounded himself with lousy actors.

AA   I don't think they were all lousy, but they were actors who were not going to give him much trouble.

IW   Did he take any trouble to try and make them any better, or did he enjoy the fact that they were considerably less good than he was?

AA   Well, he tended to bully a lot. I think he was a kind man: he certainly has a record of being very kindly. But on the stage, there was no doubt about it, he shunted people around. And when he did meet opposition – as, I believe, he did in the original production, when Ernest Milton was in it, who was a force to be reckoned with – the blood was endless. They fought and fought. I remember, Wolfit decided to wear black, and there was a scene with the papal emissary, which Ernest originally played. Ernest decided, quite shrewdly, to wear white. And all through Wolfit's big scene, all Ernest did was sit at the middle upstage in his white robes, and not a light could be seen on Wolfit. So every night – the electrician told me this, in the wings – every night, Wolfit would come off and he'd say: 'I think there's a little bit too much light on Mr Milton, you know.' And the lights went down and down and down, until it was absolutely black: and Ernest was still glowing, like life after death!

They used to have this wonderful battle at the curtain call too, because Wolfit loved to take his solo at the end. And so he used to give his sub-stars a little solo bow: on would come all the principals, bow, bow, bow, and get off as quick as they could, so there was plenty of applause left. And then the second principals, and off. And then Ernest would come on, and Ernest would stand there for hours, till they were all weakening. And Wolfit could be heard shouting from the wings: 'Ernest! Ernest! Get off Ernest! Ernest!' Wonderful stuff! I was privileged to hit the end of an era. Admittedly he was, as it were, the last of the dinosaurs; but it was marvellous to see all that, and to see him bouncing up and down in the wings, and then, at the moment of entry, to hang on to the curtain, and come round the curtain, as if exhausted from the performance; and to get the audience going: 'Oh, look, he's on his knees, poor old bugger.' 'Thank you public!' – he'd do all that bit, then bound off again for his drink. It was all tricks of the trade, but you don't see them these days.

IW   Did you learn anything useful from him?

AA   Yes, I think so. I think I learnt that theatre is show business. Some of the stuff he portrayed I didn't admire. But eventually, it's what the audience wants. He played for them. I think some would say he played to them to the exclusion of everybody else. The fact is that he hated them at the same time – a lot of artists have a love-hate relationship with their audience. But there was no doubt you'd been to the theatre when you went to see Wolfit.

IW   Did you do any technical work with his company, or are we still not there yet?

AA   No, I learnt only basic stage management, really.

IW   How long were you with Wolfit?

AA   Oh, very, very short. I was three weeks at the Edinburgh Festival. But it was like three years simply because it was a holiday job and it did give me three weeks at the Festival. And I saw so much else, because all these wonderful old actors that he employed were also past masters at getting into every show in the business without paying. So I saw all the operas and the ballets and the Piccolo Theatre of Milan – it was a very rich festival that year – not to mention all the orchestral stuff and the tattoo.

But when I got back to London, that was the whole burnt-out end, because I'd said to Wolfit that I'd go to drama school – in fact, he'd put in a word for me – and then I thought about it and thought: 'No, I don't think I can, I can't afford to.' So I didn't take that up, and obviously I couldn't go back to him. So I then took up my other loose end, my other letter of introduction, which was Robert Flemyng, who was living in Hove, I think, at the time. And I went to see him one afternoon. He was very nice, and he said: 'Well, I don't know that I can do much for you. I don't run companies like Donald Wolfit, I'm just an actor.' But he added: 'I do know Melville Gillam at Worthing and I might be able to get you a job there.' And he did get me a job of sorts. In fact, I took a salary cut from £3 a week to nothing. I went as a student ASM, and my mother sold her caravan, I remember, to pay for me. I was there for about six months. Weekly rep at Worthing had Dan Massey, Michael Bryant, Roland Curram, Ian Holm, Elizabeth Spriggs – an extraordinary collection of young actors – not to mention Peter Byrne and people like that who were there at that time. There was a welter of experienced names there that I could learn off.

I learnt all departments there. I worked for some weeks in the scenic department, didn't see the stage at all. I did a little bit of acting, two or three tiny parts. I got to be a lime operator, and I worked in the scene dock; I worked all around. I didn't do electrics but I learnt a lot more about stage management; and I was, by the time the money ran out and the season finished, fairly proficient.

Bust of Alan Ayckbourn by Keith Godwin

I then met another person who helped me. I went to see Carey Ellison of Spotlight, who's helped a lot of people, and he introduced me in turn to Hazel Vincent Wallace, who was looking for an ASM at her old Leatherhead Theatre. She was a very particular, idiosyncratic woman, who liked me very much – well, liked the look of me anyway – and engaged me as the ASM. So I went to Leatherhead. At that point, I started to do a lot more acting. She sort of took a shine to me, and if Hazel took a shine to you, you tended to get the parts.

IW   Had you been working towards this? Had you been yearning for the acting?

AA   I was looking for the acting, yes. I was a stage manager and waiting, biding my time. And I played out the rest of that year. I did quite a lot of acting: Percy in *Flare Path*, that boy in *The Rainmaker*, Jimmy Curry, and the coloured servant, Sanyamo in *South Sea Bubble*. It was weekly rep again, but I worked with a lot of good people there. Actors are quite generous people, really: they do tend to help. Sometimes it's terribly misguided help, but they're always there to say: 'If you take my tip kid, don't enter that way, it doesn't look so good.' So I was learning. I was still a long way from the technical side, but the Stage Manager there was a man called Rodney Wood; and at the end of that season, Rodney Wood, who thought for some reason that I wasn't bad at my ASM job, asked me and a part-time carpenter who was there if we'd like to come to Scarborough and form the stage team there, with me as stage manager and him as ASM. And that was the moment that I got to hear of Stephen Joseph and the theatre in the round. And one Sunday, we went up to town and we had a look at some of this man's work, although I wasn't to meet the man himself for quite a long time. We went to the Mahatma Gandhi Hall and saw a production of *Huis Clos*, which sticks out still in my mind as one of the most exciting things I've ever seen in the theatre.

IW   Was this the first time you'd encountered theatre in the round?

AA   Yes. It was an absolute knockout. It was a pretty racy play, for its time, you know. And I thought: 'This is terrific.' I also liked it because it had no scenery, and that meant less work. So we rehearsed in London that first season: again I was acting because it was a small enough company. The late Clive Goodwin was directing, and there were two actors, two actresses – Clive also acted later, and Rodney then directed. Stephen had very little to do with that season: he didn't direct. And I stage-managed with John, and there was a girl ASM, called Anne Taylor. We did our two weeks, or whatever it was in London, we went up to Scarborough and we started playing; and there was still no sign of this Stephen Joseph man. That was a great summer. I did the lights, John did the sound – that's how it started.

And eventually, Stephen turned up, this amazing bloke: he introduced himself, and he was obviously a man much more interested anyway in the technical side of the theatre than in the acting side. So we hit it off immediately: he liked our end much better. We spent a lot of time chatting about sound and how to improve it. It was all rather new, we were in the pioneering days of tape recorders. It all seemed as though it was going to be a rather brief, one-season affair. Anyway, at the end of that season a certain director from Oxford, a man called Milos Volanakis, had been up to see a couple of the shows and had liked my performances – at least, I put it down modestly to the idea that that's what he'd liked. He wanted me to audition for Oxford Playhouse, which he ran with Frank Hauser. I was always to be fated like this, to be drifting from one job to another: I never, in all my years of acting, was ever unemployed. Once I started at Worthing, I didn't stop: Worthing, Leatherhead, Scarborough, Oxford, Scarborough . . .

IW   So at what stage did you start choosing your jobs?

AA   Well, I never chose anything. Things just happened. It's this divine inertia. I went to Oxford, and again fell right into a very, very nice situation. I was very lucky there, because once again there was a big, talented company, a marvellous man running it - Frank Hauser, who was again a man genuinely interested in young talent who went out of his way to help – and it was a theatre that was on the up at the time. I suppose if I'd auditioned for it, I'd never have got in. I did *Under Milk Wood* there, and I played the romantic juve with Mai Zetterling. In fact we did a lot of exciting things that were good for a boy at that age.

   Frank Hauser was quite interested in my staying on and wanted to offer me more parts; but Stephen rang up and said: 'Do you want to come back to Scarborough and do another season?' I told Frank I was leaving, and he was very upset and said: 'Oh, why? We're offering you this and that.' And I said: 'Well, no, I think I want to go back to Scarborough. I don't know why.' So I went back and I was again acting. But I was still lumbered with this stage management which I couldn't shake off. You can get any amount of bloody actors, but stage managers are terribly rare, and people who were actually able to understand all this machinery were like gold dust. I was beginning to get quite good at it because I'd been doing it at Oxford: they'd got a tape machine there, and none of them knew how to work it.

   Stephen was beginning to introduce these winter tours, so my work pattern began to get established for the next couple of years in that I worked for thirteen weeks in the summer and then was unemployed again until about November. And then I worked through till February/March.

IW   The writing of *Square Cat*, which you wrote that winter, 1958-59, was a reaction against something. Was it a reaction against the fact that you weren't getting enough acting?

AA   Well, I didn't like the play we were in. I was doing Nicky in *Bell, Book and Candle*.

THE JOSEPH YEARS

IW   Everything one wants to say about Stephen Joseph seems to be in extremes. To those who knew him, he was a great man who inspired much love, although he never married. You've been quoted as describing him as 'half genius, half madman', which falls into the same category of extremes. Let's see if we can get any closer to pinning him down. I guess one's got to start with the objective things: Stephen, who died of cancer in 1967, was the son of Hermione Gingold and the publisher, Michael Joseph.

AA   Note the link!

IW   Yes, indeed, your mother's friend; though that coincidence played no part in either your meeting or your work with Stephen. I suppose objectively now, one can see a lot of theatres that he was very much responsible for. He founded, obviously, the theatre in the round in Scarborough, though he never saw the one that you're now in. He founded the Victoria Theatre at Stoke-on-Trent which Peter Cheeseman now directs; in fact, he converted it with his own hands to a large extent. Those are the two theatres he actually founded. But his hand obviously can be seen very much, too, in Manchester University Theatre, on which he worked as consultant; in the Nuffield Studio at Lancaster University; and I would think there's very little doubt that neither the Bolton Octagon nor the Royal Exchange Theatre in Manchester, neither the Cottesloe nor the Warehouse, nor perhaps the Other Place of the RSC, could have come into being, had Stephen Joseph not done what he did.

AA   Yes, I would think that's true. I have the very clear impression that when I started in the theatre, there weren't any other sorts of theatres than proscenium arches. Stephen was a lone voice in the wilderness, and certainly in my experience – and I did go to a lot of theatre at that time – seeing theatre in the round at the Mahatma Gandhi Hall was the first time I had seen any sort of theatre other than a conventional proscenium arch. I believe there must have been end-stages around, but there certainly weren't in-the-rounds; I'm sure there weren't even thrust stages. And he certainly opened up, in many people's minds, the alternatives. He was an extremist for the round, but then he was, as you said, an extremist about everything. But I think being a pioneer makes you extreme: you have to take an extreme point of view in order to get your point across. He said: 'Theatre in the round is the only sort of theatre', and you know he didn't actually believe it.

Though he intensely disliked the pros. He really did. And I think he didn't like – as I don't actually like – the compromises that came up: the thrust stages. He believed that you should go the full round or not at all. He marched down St. James's, you know, when Olivier and Vivien Leigh were marching, saying: 'Save the St. James's theatre'. He marched the other way, saying: 'Pull down the St. James's (and build a more sensible theatre in the basement of an office block that'll pay the rates).' Which didn't make him very popular. But he very much believed that all new theatres should self-destruct in seven years, which was his other great maxim. I think he meant the personnel as much as anything.

The Stephen Joseph Theatre in the Round, Scarborough

IW   One of Stephen's claimed reasons for getting so deeply into theatre in the round was economy, of course. At the time that he was starting the theatre company neither he nor his friends had enough money to do anything else. Is that believable?

AA   I think it is. He was Jewish as well and he was very clever with his pennies. He was well aware of the economics of theatre in the round. We've blessed him ever since for it, because, although our budgets are certainly horrific when compared with the ones he used to work with, I still suspect that a larger part is spent upon the most important element, which is the human element, than in any other sort of theatre. We have less need for the material trappings. If you've got a great big stage to fill, you've got to fill it. The audience will get very annoyed if you don't have a few scenic flats around occasionally. And I think he was very clever in that sense, that he was able to produce theatre that didn't lose quality by cheeseparing.

IW   But his love for the round was not based upon economics.

AA   It wasn't based on that, I don't think. I think it was based upon the immediacy of it. His great concept – and this is something he did say a thousand times – was that the only thing that mattered about theatre, when it came to it, was the actor and the audience. This was the most important concept and the round, more than any other medium, emphasises this most strongly. The actor is in the middle and the audience surrounds him, and there's nothing else there, really.

IW   There's something of a paradox there, isn't there, that the man who believed that theatre was – in the expression he used in an article – 'a passionate affair between the actor and his audience,' should in fact get into the position of founding a writers' theatre. The writer, the director, were both relegated to secondary positions as far as he was concerned, and yet here he was: the man who gave Pinter the chance to get *The Birthday Party* going after its first flop; the man who gave Ayckbourn his first chance. And David Campton was, I suppose, the house dramatist when you went in?

AA   Yes, he was. And an occasional was James Saunders who was very new then: I think we did his very first play, *Alas, Poor Fred*. Yes, Stephen was full of paradoxes like that. But then he wasn't a great one for improvisation – you know, where actor and audience say: 'Well, stuff the dramatist, let's get on and create our own stuff.' He held one or two rather half-hearted improvisation classes when I was there, but they were mainly to improve the art of the actor, not to replace the dramatist; although he would always emphasise that the dramatist, in the last analysis, was serving the actor, which I think is right – eventually the audience, whether they like it or not, are watching the actor and not the dramatist. They're watching the dramatist through the actor, and if you don't get your actor right, there's very few dramatists who can actually survive.

IW   Would it be fair to say that he wasn't a man particularly interested in the ideas of plays? It's hard to imagine him, for example, doing a George Devine, who, at roughly the same time, was running a very different sort of writers' theatre at the Royal Court.

AA   He had rather strange tastes in plays. One of his favourite plays was Houseman's *Victoria Regina* which he thought was a wonderful play and was an unashamedly romantic piece: the old queen dying, waving. I once found I was playing Prince Albert in that and I described it as a load of rubbish, I remember, at some heated rehearsal. He got very white and said: 'This is my favourite play and I won't have that.' I said: 'I'm frightfully sorry.'

But, at the other end, he was a great supporter of the new drama, and John Whiting, I know, he was mad about. He was very excited by all the new stuff coming along: the Osbornes and so on.

IW   You described first getting to know Stephen more or less over the sound console, because you were both in the nuts and bolts of the theatre. In his book, *Theatre in the Round*, he's writing about the appointment of Joan Macalpine as Manager, who wanted to come into the company because she wanted to write plays. He said: 'Would-be playwrights are two a penny, but Joan could drive the green lorry.' One suspects that this side of theatre was actually more exciting to him than anything that happened on the stage.

AA   Joan tells the story of her interview with him. He was such a shy man when you first met him, he always stared at his blotter; and she, being a sort of early liberationist, was J. Macalpine, so she signed herself 'J. Macalpine'. And there really wasn't any indication as to her sex. And she sat there nodding and not getting a word out while he outlined the job: 'Well, I expect you to do this, and I expect you to do that, and I expect you'll want to do that, and I see you've got a licence, and so on. Can I offer you the job?' And she said: 'Oh, thank you.' And he looked up in total amazement and saw a woman. I don't know how true it is, but it is quite possible for Stephen to have done that. I know he auditioned one actor, and he engaged him purely on the strength of his walking in when his gramophone was playing. Stephen said: 'What is this music?' And the actor frowned and said: 'Bach.' He said: 'Right, yes, well you start on Tuesday.'

IW   Yes, he claimed that he never auditioned an actor: he always interviewed them. He also made a claim that he never directed plays: he only trained actors.

AA   That's right. I've been in several of his productions and can vouch for that. His claim – and it was quite a legitimate one in many senses – was that in theatre in the round, particularly when two or three alone were gathered together on stage, it was quite possible, if the set was reasonably well laid out, to allow the scene to take its course. Which is fine, except that this did rely on the fact that they were all experienced actors, all tremendously equal in terms of generosity, and so on – and of course, as one knows, you do need something a little stronger. Which is why I suspect – although there were moments in his productions when they worked very well — I would say he wasn't the strongest of directors.

He knew more than any person I've ever known about playwriting, when it came to talking about it, and he knew more about directing than any living person, and I suspect he knew an awful lot about acting: he certainly managed to talk about it very lucidly and entertainingly and interestingly, although he must have been the world's worst actor. So he was a teacher and not a doer. He was a doer in other senses, but it was always to do with the fringe things: putting the noticeboards up in the foyer, and designing the new theatre. I always felt that Stephen's mind was on higher things than the performances. They were rather small beer in Stephen's game: he was on another plane.

Alan Ayckbourn with Stanley Page and Peter King in Harold Pinter's *The Collection* at Stoke-on-Trent

IW He said of your *Mr. Whatnot*: 'The play made a pointing gesture in the direction of anarchy.' Which is an interesting reflection, because he always called himself an anarchist. He was a sort of benevolent anarchist and profoundly distrustful of authority, which is why he didn't actually believe in the business of directing, but rather in the business of encouraging actors to act (which didn't always work). I wonder whether there was at that stage any sort of meeting of minds between you on this?

AA Yes, I suppose so. I always think of the *Whatnot* theme as being the Id figure who bounds along, the one inside me that would like to up-end and destroy – not destroy gratuitously, just to up-end, really, and confuse a little, upset *status quos*. And I suppose Stephen was much of a oneness with that anyway. I always liked the way he would leave many a meeting in uproar. He did awful things: he used to insult the press regularly, which any theatre manager will tell you is not a very good idea. When it comes to your next meeting, there's a lot of very injured men dipping their pens into something rather violent! The other thing he used to do was to invite them all to tea, which was also not a very good idea. They'd all arrive, ready for a nice stiffening bracer and find themselves faced with biscuits and cups; because he was teetotal completely. Well, he got drunk with me once. Somebody gave him a bottle of whisky as a 'thank you very much' present, and he said: 'Here's a bottle of whisky. Would you like to share it with me?' And he really did drink like a non-drinker: he poured himself half a tumbler and swilled away. I had some water with mine, but he drank three-quarters of a bottle; and he suddenly fell off his chair. 'Do you know, Ayckers, I'm completely pissed.'

We spent a lot of time together. When he was ill – and he was quite a lot with various things – I used to cart round my portable gramophone and play him all my corny old records. He used to say: 'Oh dear, oh dear, have you got any chamber music?' But I used to play him all my Tchaikovskys. Always when he was in bed he used to decide to make a new cardboard theatre – the ultimate theatre in the round. He was into the sort of things we're still talking about – walk-around grids and so on. But he was also into two-storey theatre, and I'm still looking at the idea. In *Taking Steps* I came near to it, but I decided to set it on one floor. His idea was to have two floors, so the play could take place on two levels. And he worked out that it could be done in the theatre structurally, with perfect sightlines in the round. Hell of a difficult thing to build, though.

Then he got into fish-and-chip theatre, and that was really beyond me. My instincts as an actor were such that I couldn't bear the thought of people eating fish and chips all around me when I was trying to give my performance. But he did promise that they'd be behind glass. And they'd have you amplified – in which case, to me it seemed you were better off on television.

IW He felt the natural theatre critics – the real theatre critics – were the holidaymakers at

Mr. Whatnot programme cover for the opening of the Scarborough company's permanent theatre

Mr Whatnot

Alan Ayckbourn

Cayton Bay, who talked through the bits they found boring and sat absolutely rapt through the bits which made them absolutely rapt. It doesn't seem to me to hold a great deal of future for the playwright at all.

AA   Well no, it's rather like children's theatre, in the sense that you've got to keep the action going. I think theatre is actually a very thinking art: you have to go with your brain fairly clear and be prepared to give it quite a lot of attention. Half the joys in theatre are often in being stimulated sufficiently by the dramatist, either because of the ideas he puts out or simply, for example in the case of *Taking Steps*, because of the fact that you have got to grasp the concept of three floors; and having grasped it, enjoying that in much the same way you might enjoy an executive toy. Nonetheless, you can't really afford to be knackered from a day digging trenches, when all you actually want is to put your feet up, have a pint of beer and be sung to by a lady with big boobs. I remember Tony Church saying: '*King Lear* takes an enormous amount of work and effort; and of course there will always be people who do a hard day's work who will want to go to the theatre and see it, and who will very much enjoy it. But not the majority of people.' And I know when I've done a bloody hard day, the last thing I want to do is go and see *King Lear*. I want to watch something really vulgar on telly. And by very vulgar, I mean something very simple and very colourful and great fun, preferably American, with a lot of cars going round corners on two wheels.

IW   But the fact is that most of those who do go to the theatre have got to go after a day's work, because there's no way we can take a day off work just to prepare ourselves for the business of going to the theatre.

AA   Yes; that's why when we put the word 'comedy' after the title, many more people go than to a 'a drama'. But the other side of the coin is that I think the theatre has a great responsibility: it is not sufficient for plays to sit there and say: 'Come and get me.' You've got to go out and get the audience, and I think there is an entertainment quotient which plays ought to contain. The best ones, I think, do. Shakespeare's plays are highly entertaining if they're produced half well. Usually the story's quite sufficient to keep you going on the best ones, and if you happen also to be a freak for language and metaphor and all sorts of other things, you can get into that as well. But there's a dramatist who actually knew that he'd got down in his pit a lot of guys who'd done a hard day's work, and needed to be entertained on a fairly basic level. That's not to insult them, merely to acknowledge when they say: 'God, mate, I can hardly hear one word in three: make the plot simple tonight.' And that was very important.

IW   If you extend that a little bit further, you get into circus, don't you?

AA   Yes, but then you throw away the other bit. Yes, you do get into circus – but I think that's what Stephen used to preach. He had a very strong feeling towards fish-and-chip theatre on the one hand, and yet he did grasp quite difficult plays.

IW   How did Stephen come to be in Scarborough?

AA   The story goes that he was in search of premises in which to establish a theatre in the round for longer than one night – which is what he was doing at the Mahatma Gandhi. He obviously was looking outside London. I think he got as far as Leeds for some reason, and he met John Wood, who was the Education Officer, who tipped him off that the library in Scarborough had a rather good, although shortly-to-out-go, Chief Librarian called Colley, who was quite sympathetic. Stephen zoomed over, met Colley, outlined what he wanted to do – which was six or eight weeks of new plays, in the summer, using a couple of the rooms up there on the first floor of the library. And Colley, who was obviously a man of some vision and imagination, but who was also on the verge of retirement, so probably had less to lose than a man who was coming into the job said: 'Fine!' And Stephen moved in there. PB's story (she was his housekeeper) is that the company all came up and stayed in one house. He advertised for her, actually, in the paper, and she came along.

IW   She was living on a houseboat at the time, wasn't she?

AA   That's right. She'd never cooked before for anyone.

IW   I think it's worth just establishing her. She was Veronica Pemberton-Billing.

AA   She was another person he took completely on trust. She was a wonderful woman, the widow of Pemberton-Billing the MP. Her past is slightly shadowy, in that she never said much about it, just little anecdotes. But she had a very colourful marriage with a very colourful man. She was a slim, very beautiful girl, obviously a flapper of some quality, who got involved with gun-running and everything else that Pemberton-Billing got into – all his court cases and all the scandals – and adored him, absolutely. And she said she was an absolutely silly: you know, she couldn't open a door unless somebody did it for her. She'd certainly never cooked, since she used to sit around on sofas, eating bonbons and being patted by the big man. Then he died quite suddenly, and she, knowing her terrible irresponsibility with money, put it all into a trust which gave her, at the time, an adequate but quite restrictive income which forced her to go out to work.

She answered Stephen's advertisement. I don't know if she'd done anything before that; I think not. He took her on because he liked her – she grew rather large rather quickly after her husband's death – took her up to Scarborough, gave her the house that he'd taken for the summer, in which all the actors were living, and said: 'Cook us a meal by one o'clock.'

And they all went off to rehearse; and she ran around in absolute panic. Two of the actresses had children, so she had those there as well – she had someone to help her with them. All she knew was that if you got a joint, and put some fat with it and stuffed it in a tin and put it in the oven, it would cook in time – how long, she didn't know. The company all came home at lunch-time and it was all right. And over that summer, she said, she learnt how to cook, she learnt how to housekeep and she also was absolutely captivated by Stephen, and remained so.

IW   She was sort of Mother Superior for the whole company, wasn't she? She called herself the Mother Hen.

AA   She was. The only thing you could really do to upset PB was ever to criticise Stephen in her presence. She was just like a dog with its master. And he used to treat her appallingly. He would think nothing of breezing in about eleven, saying: 'Hello, PB. I've brought eight people in for supper.' 'Yes, Stephen,' she'd say. She'd chase around; and in a way, she loved it. She would sit there, nodding in on his conversations, and he treated her in an affectionate, but fairly patronising way: pat her on the head and say: 'Yes, well done, PB: off to bed.' She'd do anything for the man, and indeed nursed him in his last days. She was wonderful.

IW   The work pattern when you joined Stephen was twelve weeks in Scarborough in the summer.

AA   Yes it was, by the time I joined: it was their third year. There was a two-weekly pattern, and we put on an awful lot of plays. No – the first year I was there, it was three weeks, because it was only four plays we did; but he did step it up after that. We did do six or eight: it was quite heavy, and it was quite hard work. You didn't get a lot of time off in Stephen's day.

IW   What was the work? I'm never clear. He didn't rehearse you.

AA   Well, we did rehearse, but he wasn't particularly involved. He'd sit there jogging one leg and making notes about something else – except when he was doing other things. I remember dress rehearsals where he was actually drilling in the auditorium, putting up new bannister rails. And we were screaming about the bloody din and saying: 'Could you keep it down please, Stephen, we're trying to dress rehearse!' 'Well, you won't get anybody in tonight, people, unless these bannister rails are secure.' So you'd carry on desperately against odds like that. One got the sense that in general he found rehearsals extremely boring. I had occasion to sit next to him in rehearsals when he was doing my play. He said: 'Oh, for a team of trained acrobats, or something! Oh, that these people could get on with it!' I said: 'Well, you know, they're doing their best: they've only just dropped their books.' I don't think he had time for all that, really. He liked the first bit of rehearsal and the last bit: it was the middle bit which was the one which caused the black hole where everything disappears.

IW   There's an impression one has that he was almost running a constant seminar with you in the earlier days – not you personally, but with the company. Is that right?

AA   Yes. He believed that all of us shouldn't be purely concerned with our own little role in theatre, that theatre people should be total theatre people. That, in fact, if you were an actor, that didn't mean that you didn't know about the box office. In fact, on the contrary, you *should* know how ticket stubs were dealt with. I found it invaluable that he would not think it peculiar that an actor should work the sound. In fact, if an actor was interested in the sound, then it seemed a very good reason for him to work it; and if necessary, one would re-write the play, in order that he could work it — give him an early exit so he could play the music. He was very flexible to that extent.

IW   And to that extent, if you hadn't had that sort of training, most of your plays you couldn't have written, because most of them are based in stage management of one sort or another.

AA   I adore lighting and I love sound; and he encouraged both aspects. He found that admirable that somebody should have those interests. And one regrets – I do, and I'm sure he would – the demarcations which have happened in the theatre, by necessity. Very few actors ever go up into the control box nowadays, whereas it would then have been a natural thing for half the cast to be up there at any one time, because they were probably doing something of importance up there.

IW   Did you drive the green lorry?

AA   No, I was not a driver at that time. I used to 'mate' with Joan Macalpine, if you'll pardon the expression. She drove, and the only thing she wasn't able to do was to put the handbrake on. She wasn't strong enough for that, and so I used to stand up, and she'd say: 'Brake!' suddenly – and, two-handed, I'd hoick the thing up, which was actually beyond her, and let it off again.

IW   Because, after your summer season in Scarborough, you went out on the road, right?

AA   Yes.

IW   How much of this did you do? How many years of this?

AA   Two or three. I did the Leicester-Birmingham-Hemel Hempstead-Harlow run quite a lot.

IW   Did you go to Wellingborough?

AA   I directed the three plays for Wellingborough, yes.

IW   What were they? Camptons, were they?

AA   Yes. Oscar Quitak and Pat England were in them, and I was in them; and there was a total disaster area of a stage manager called Kenneth Colley, who went on to become an extremely good actor, but he was a man who claimed to know all there was to know about tape recorders.

IW   Last seen as Jesus Christ, incidentally, in *The Life of Brian*.

AA   Yes. A wonderful actor. Out of work, came along, got the job because he was the only one who applied for it – Stephen, I think, advertised it in a window in Soho, or something. Anyway, this guy turned up. I said: 'Can you operate a Brenell tape deck?' 'Oh yes, yes.' Right. You could tell as soon as he stared at it that he'd absolutely never seen a tape deck in his life before. So, technically, in Wellingborough the show was a disaster. I could hear him winding to and fro, looking for cues, as we vamped our way through a play Campton had written which had, I suppose, almost as many sound effects as *Mr. Whatnot*. It was riddled with them: a play called *Out of the Flying Pan*.

But my great moment of touring with Stephen was Hemel Hempstead. We were playing in the Adeyfield Hall, and there was one Wednesday when the place was needed for a dance. Anyway, Stephen, not to be done out of this performance, had booked us into the Standard Telephone and Cables Company, or some such, for a performance of a different play, for that evening. This entailed us taking down the entire auditorium — all those touring rostra, all the set – loading the lorries, driving over to this telephone place, setting it up to do *Dial M For Murder* for one night, taking it down again, driving it back and dumping it that night. The crew to put it up was Stephen, Rodney Wood (the manager), John Smith and I, who were the stage management, and one rather limp girl, who didn't do very much really, except stand there and wave her arms. We guessed four of us could put it up in two hours. But there were only two of us, because Stephen's van had broken down in London and Rodney had broken down somewhere else. So John and I had to put the whole auditorium together on our own; we'd arrived at ten and we finished at two. We hadn't lit the show. The matinee was at 2.30, the actors had turned up and we said: 'What are the bookings?' And the bookings were two people – who were parents of one of the cast, so we couldn't cancel the show. So I remember I went in to the dressing room and said: 'I'm terribly sorry, I think we're going to go mad, so we're going home. Can you do the show with no stage management; we'll just put all the lights on.' 'Certainly,' said the actors, realising we were very near a crisis. So we went home and had a bath, and they did the show. They welcomed the audience individually as they came in, sat them down and did the show to them. And that, I think, was my low spot of Stephen Joseph touring! He turned up at three saying: 'Sorry, people! Got it up, have you? Well done!'

IW   Did you ever count the number of rostrums that there were?

AA   Oh God, there were hundreds!

IW   They were heavy, I know.

AA   Yes. And there were a lot of them. He also had – which we didn't put up this day – a portable grid; a sort of thing like a flying bedstead, which was built out of scaffolding poles, locked together with Allen keys, and which stood in a rigid structure on which you hung your lamps in a square round the acting area. I remember at one place the grid arrived, and he said: 'This is going to be exciting: we're going to erect it now.' And we erected this thing, or we tried to, with everyone holding on to one foot of it, and it didn't stand up. It was unstable. For once, Stephen's mathematics and engineering brain had totally left him. This thing swayed and it hurtled: to let the public in would have been fatal, without even hanging a lamp on it. He was undeterred: he sat down in the middle of the room. We were holding on to these poles, saying: 'Come on, Stephen, for Christ's sake, it's falling down!' He said: 'Just a minute, people!' And he re-designed the existing structure, like a kid with a Meccano set. We then rushed around and built eight separate towers: and that, with modifications, became the basis of the touring kit.

IW   You were touring what – weekly? Or fortnightly?

AA   We were doing a show a week. We used to take about four plays out. There was a distinguished time when, I remember, we opened with a Campton, then we played one of mine, then we played another Campton, then we played another of mine: it really was like ducks and drakes. Sometimes we had even more in the repertoire: we did seem to have an awful lot of plays going around at that time. It was a very small company, certainly the first tour we did: two girls and three men, plus me as an acting ASM and an acting girl ASM.

IW   And you did all the plays in each place?

AA   Yes. We did four weeks. But then in Leicester we went to two or three venues, because we were only there for one week in each.

IW   And dismantling all this kit all the time?

AA   Yes, we totally dismantled it all. Stoke was one of the nicest places: we played in the Municipal Hall at Newcastle-under-Lyme, which was lovely, except it was upstairs. But once up there, it was this big, big, big room, and I think some of the happiest memories of touring were there. There was a lovely big kitchen, and PB was a great house mother. She used to make huge bowls of soup; there was always food after the show.

IW   She was cooking not only for the company, but for the audiences as well. She used to make the most amazing cakes for every performance, didn't she?

AA   That's right. But to the hungry ones of us, of which I was one of the most, she would always tip the wink and say: 'There's some sausage rolls in there if you want them.' And it was very much a family thing. We used to strike Scarborough Saturday night and drive through the night then to Leicester, and arrive there some time on Sunday, snatch some sleep and then start setting up for a performance on Monday. There was no messing around. I remember arriving in Leicester, and sleeping on David Campton's floor. We crept into the house, and we ran out of rooms. Somebody had nipped in and shut the door, and Stephen and I were left in the sitting room; and we split the cushions, and lay end to end in the sitting room. And he said: 'Would you like my feet or my boots?' I said: 'I think I'll have your boots tonight.' I went to sleep with these great big, size 12 boots near my face.

IW   You were telling me how you came to write *Square Cat*. You were getting sick of playing Nicky in *Bell, Book and Candle*, you said, by John van Druten. Now what was Stephen's role in getting you to write?

AA   He said to me: 'If you want a better part, you'd better write one for yourself. Write a play, I'll do it. If it's any good.' And I said: 'Fine.' And he said: 'Write yourself a main part' – which was actually a very shrewd remark, because presumably, if the play had not worked at all, there was no way I as an actor was going to risk my neck in it. So at least I had to have reasonable confidence in it. It was during that first tour, and it was in the digs on the tour that I wrote *Square Cat*. It was untypical of me in that firstly, it was written over quite a long period, and secondly, it was written with a great deal of help from Christine – structurally, not dialogue-wise. She was very helpful. We talked out: 'What if . . . ? What if . . . ? What if . . . ? How about trying it this way round?' And it was very much an exercise, in the sense that we were trying to get effects.

IW   Christine's your wife, and she was an actress in the company.

AA   Yes.

IW   Did you go back to Stephen with it a lot as well?

AA   Only when it was finished, I went to him then. He did very Stephenesque things: he scribbled huge examples of the dialogue he thought ought to have taken place in the margin, which were awful. And then he got very upset. He said: 'You didn't use any of my dialogue;' and I said: 'Well, it didn't quite fit my style, Stephen, but it was very good.'

I was aware that he'd had a very strange effect on David Campton. Stephen had very strong ideas, although he couldn't actually put them into practice, about plays. He didn't necessarily give David the plots, but he certainly encouraged and channelled his writing towards what was then the comedy of menace school, and threw in his thoughts on nuclear disasters. Campton was for some years one of the front runners of comedy of menace. But

Alan Ayckbourn with David Campton in *Love After All*

49

he also had another strand to his writing, which was a much more romantic and, I think, a much more human strand, which he suppressed – plays like *Cactus Garden*. I'm never quite sure how David's talent would have developed, had he been allowed not to be quite so strongly dominated by Stephen saying: 'This is what I want, David; can you write it?'

The only time Stephen tried that with me was on *Dad's Tale*, when I learnt quite an object lesson. He wanted me to collaborate with David; and David wrote a synopsis for *Dad's Tale*, based on *The Borrowers*. By the time I got it, I found I was unable actually to work to other people's ideas. I was maybe too undisciplined, I don't know; so I totally went my own way.

Then again Stephen tried to stick his oar in with *Standing Room Only*. By this time he was getting into over-population: he decided if the human race didn't destroy itself, it was going to over-breed. He said – and this is typical of Stephen's suggestions – would I like to write about that? I hadn't really thought about it. He outlined his plot, which was set on Venus, where the population was now expanding because Earth had over-populated. And I wrestled around trying to get up a Venus setting, but realised that by the time you'd established (*a*) what life was like on Venus, and (*b*) what life was like being over-populated, there wasn't anything left for the play to do, except just tie it up rather neatly: somebody could possibly drop dead in the last five minutes. So I re-set it in Shaftesbury Avenue in a bus – which actually turned out to be the best bit of the idea. Everything else got rather tedious, although the play worked quite well. I think. All the technical details of the over-population got a bit swamped in the more interesting things, which were the human relationships, as they always are. I saw a warning light then that Stephen's ideas, although exciting, were not for me, because they actually didn't lead me anywhere. I was having to re-think them quite radically. And by the time I'd got to *Mr. Whatnot*, which was written totally independently of him, I had nothing directly whatever to do with him, in terms of writing, except the residue of his ideas – obviously that was still there.

IW   Let's go back to *The Square Cat*. You delivered the script to him. How did he react to it initially?

AA   He read it very quickly. My impression always was that he flipped the script through with his thumb, in some mysterious way, and was able to tell you immediately what was wrong with it – a little bit cavalier to a writer who's spent hours on it. He was usually right. In the case of *Square Cat* he had quite good suggestions to make – he always did. I got to learn later that suggestions he made about the structure were invariably right, about the content or 'a nice joke to go in here' invariably wrong, because he wasn't actually good at penning *bons mots*: they used to fall very flat, and if he put them in at rehearsal, you were always well advised to take them out again for performance. But, in this case, he structured the play for me again, although he didn't do anything radical: he cut it – he always cut everything quite ruthlessly – and left it then to production.

IW   What was the play about?

AA   It was about a family – it sounds terribly banal – about a husband, his wife, his son and his daughter. The mother has got an obsession with a pop singer. She's fallen in love with him from a distance, thinks he's wonderful and swoony. She therefore rents a house in the country – (a little Anouilh coming out there: there were a lot of definite influences in this play. In fact it's *Dinner With The Family*, I now realise!) – in order to invite the pop singer down for a marvellous weekend with her. And she was going to pretend to be someone totally different; have no family, and be a rich woman – she'd arranged it all. The family, having got wise to this, followed her down.

I don't quite know why he comes, but anyway he agrees to come, we find out later. The family has followed her down and is not going to let mother get away as easily as that. They say: 'All right, let him come.' She's very cross and says: 'No, you've spoiled the whole thing.' He turns up – that's me – and of course he's not at all the glittering figure of the silver screen, but shy and bespectacled and wanting a quiet time – and this he thought was it. And he's horrified to see that mother is a sort of elderly groupie. The family roars with merriment saying: 'Look, you see, look at your hero. He's really nothing very much.' At which point he bounds out and comes back again in glitter costume, twanging his guitar, saying: 'OK, this is war' – or words to that effect (I can't remember much of the plot). He gets together with the daughter eventually, and romance blossoms there. Mother finds the error of her ways and goes back to her husband. Jerry Ross finds true love with the simple girl, and all fades into the sunset. I don't think it was very good as a play, looking back on it, but it was OK for a first one. It's not one that one would ever want to see done again.

IW   You managed all that with nary a twang of the guitar, and not a sung word?

AA   It was so silly. I did actually set myself as an actor an impossible task, yes. I did originally play a guitar, and sing a song, and dance – none of which I do at all well. A bloke called Donny taught me about five chords, in order that I could sing 'I gave my love a cherry', which seemed a nice, extremely boring, morose song which goes on for ages. But even that I used to have very great difficulty with. I used to sing it on some nights –whenever PB was in, she would insist I sang it – but on other nights, I would nod vaguely in the direction of the lighting box and they'd take the lights out rather swiftly; so I would just play one open chord – sploing – and the lights would go. And other nights I would sing, excruciatingly, 'I gave my love a cherry' to a rather flat guitar, because I hadn't actually learnt to tune it.

IW   Was this a light comedy?

AA   It was farce. I think it comes under the term farce, because there was a lot of leaping

51

about and mistaken identities in it. It was certainly as broad as I got for quite some time. It was curious, because I didn't sit down to write anything particularly, except a play. I'd been writing before that, but they'd never had the test of production, and most of them, with a couple of exceptions which had been rather morose pieces, had been comic in tone.

IW Had Stephen seen those?

AA He'd seen some of them. He'd seen my Pirandello play, which was the one that everyone writes, about the group of actors with a director, and they all take on the characters – and he said: 'Yes, that's a Pirandello play!' I said: 'Yes it is.' And I think I'd probably got a Ionesco play as well. I was very influenced by Ionesco.

IW So you'd done all this before *Square Cat*?

AA Yes.

IW And what was the reaction to *Square Cat* once it got on the stage? Did the audiences come, in the first place?

AA Yes, they came a lot. I don't know what it did in terms of percentage: it made me forty-seven quid, I remember, more than I earned in several weeks. It proved very popular because it was what it was – a farce, with no pretensions to anything else – and it did give people quite a laugh. And I think Stephen did recognise, if nothing else, that he'd found a writer who, nurtured a little, could possibly keep his box office afloat, allowing David, who was running in parallel with me, a chance to develop his less commercial style – because he had distinctly two. Stephen was much more keen for David to get on with his *Four Minute Warnings* and his *View from The Brinks*, continuing with *Lunatic Views*, than his commercial stuff. I was left rather in the position of being encouraged to carry on writing, in the hope of bringing in an audience; which I did, for the next two or three plays.

IW And *Love After All* was asked for, was it?

AA Yes. Stephen directed *Square Cat*; *Love After All* was done by Clifford Williams. But at some period when it was touring, I went off to do National Service, and I left the company.

IW Right, come on, we'd better have that out!

AA I'd been pursued by these awful men to do National Service for years. They started when I was seventeen, I was now about nineteen.

Alan Ayckbourn as the guitar-toting pop singer in his first play, *The Square Cat*

IW   Nineteen, with a wife and two kids?

AA   Right – one kid, anyway, yes. There were rumours that National Service was finishing. In fact, it *was* finishing. But they're remorseless, these chaps, and they eventually cornered me in Scarborough. They had a sort of interview/exam and a medical. It was a pretty idiot exam, saying things like: 'You stop the car with: A Horn, A Rear Bumper or A Brake. Please tick the box you think is the correct one.' I was desperately trying to avoid this, so I thought: 'Well, if I can get qualified as an absolute moron, I might not get in.' So I ticked 'Rear Bumper'. It was rather sweet, because there was a guy next to me – a wonderful, big, thick fellow – who was desperate to get in. His ambition was to be a serving officer in some army – that would be his ideal. He'd spotted me as the genius around the place, and was cribbing off me. And I thought: 'Oh god, he's copying down my answers.' I was shaking my head and pointing to the correct answer, and he was laughing and was actually copying down half my answers, and then trying to correct me when he'd obviously spotted something – he obviously knew it was 'Brake'. So we had this embarrassing exchange, in which I'm sure I failed him: I got two right by mistake, actually.

IW   But they passed you because they thought you had a sense of humour?

AA   They passed me. I went in and this chap said: 'Well, ah, Mr. Ayckbourn, you've scored an absolute total of two in the intelligence test, which is something of a record.' I said: 'Oh yes?' He said: 'Oh, but you do appear to have two A levels and so I think we can dispense with the intelligence test. Why do you want to join the RAF?' I said: 'Well, the real reason is that they don't wear boots, they wear shoes.' He said: 'Well, that is a reason for joining. It's not a very strong one.' I said: 'I hear you do less bull.' He said: 'Yes, we do.' Then he did their wonderful old trick. 'Look, here are your options as a National Service-man joining the RAF,' he said, pulling down a screen. 'You can be one of the following: a clerk, or a male nurse. I think that's it. If you wanted to sign for three years – I mean, just for the extra year – you could be a fighter pilot! You see, the options do get somewhat wider.' And I said: 'Oh yes, yes they do. I think I'll stick with the National Service options.' He said: 'Well, male nurse?' And I said: 'Well, I do faint at the sight of blood.' He said: 'Well, it's down to clerk, then, isn't it?' I said: 'Yes, that'll be fine. I don't mind being a clerk at all. I'd quite like being a clerk, really.'

So, some months later, I got notice to join up. I did contemplate trying to break my foot in the lift, to get out of going. I actually lost my nerve, so I just got very, very drunk that night, said: 'Farewell for two years, dear wife, dear baby,' and she went home to her parents, because I certainly wasn't going to see them for my eight weeks basic training. I caught the train and we got to Cardington. We roared into the camp in a lorry, and were marshalled into a hut with these other lads, most of whom were slightly younger than I was – I was getting on. This bloke was sitting there and he said: 'Well, first of all, chaps, let's just establish how long you are all signing for? Dawkins?' 'Five years, sir.' 'Nine years, sir.' 'Ten years, sir.' 'Seven years, sir.' I thought: 'Christ, what is this?' He said: 'I don't seem to have your name.' I said: 'Ayckbourn, sir.' 'No, it's not on here. How long are you signing on for?' I said: 'As short as possible.' He said: 'Are you a Regular?' I said: 'National Service.' He said: 'Well, you shouldn't be in here, this is a Regular intake. You can't sleep in a hut with Regulars.' So I was segregated, as if I had some awful, man-eating disease, and I was put in a hut on my own, a 48-bed hut. He said: 'Light the fire if you want to: here is some wood.' It was bloody freezing: it was January. So I took the blankets off about eight other beds and piled them over me, and lay in bed. I'd read the notice: *Reveille is at six o'clock. All men will be standing outside their huts in full uniform.* I hadn't got any uniform. I thought: 'Christ, how am I going to get up at six?' So I put my watch by my bed and I went to sleep.

When I woke up, I looked at my watch: it said half past eight! I'd actually missed Reveille! I'd seen films, you know, where everyone marched up and down with heavy packs for punishment, being shot at! So I got out of bed and I thought I'd better put things right. I looked at the notice, and it said: *Kit inspection is at 9, and all beds will be folded, with their blankets 8 centimetres from the edge and* – you know – *three folds from the middle and the seam down the left hand side . . .* ' I was reading this, and I suddenly realised that I'd stripped eight or ten beds, so I was going to have to make up ten beds in this extraordinary way. I started on this, and in came a corporal. He said: 'Morning!' I said: 'Look, I'm extremely sorry. I just overslept, and I genuinely didn't hear the bugle or anything.' He said: 'Well, I looked in on you at six, and you looked very peaceful, so I left you.' I said: 'Oh! Well that was very nice of you. Is there anything I should be doing?' He said: 'Well, no, you can go to the NAAFI. Report back here at eleven. Should be some other lads arriving. Then you can be part of that.' I said: 'Oh, thank you very much, Corporal.' So I went across to the NAAFI and had breakfast. And I came back at eleven and I sat in my hut, and about a quarter to twelve another corporal came in. He said: 'What are you doing here?' I said: 'I'm waiting for the other corporal, who's probably gone out to meet these other men, you see.' He said: 'Well, don't hang around in here. Look, go to the NAAFI. Come back here at one.' So I said to him: 'Yes, right, thank you very much, Corporal.' I went back in the NAAFI; and this went on most of the day. Every time I came back, he said: 'Don't sit around in your hut, go over to the NAAFI'. I was bloated with awful NAAFI food.

The next thing that happened was that he said: 'You're all right, now. There's some lads arriving. They're Glaswegians, and there's forty-seven of them.' I said: 'Oh. Oh, goodness!' And he said: 'No, I don't think that's a very good idea. No. I'll tell you what. No, not the Glaswegians. There's another lot. You're responsible, you look an educated sort of bloke. I want you to look after a feller. He's, you know, he's a bit . . . ' I said: 'Ah, is he? Yes, right.' He said: 'He's a Maltese.' And I said: 'Ah yes, yes.' He said: 'He was a Pilot Officer in the Maltese Air Force, and he's got this thing about starting again in the Royal Air Force as an ordinary aircraftsman. He feels he should. And there's no way, because Maltese is rubbish, you know. And he's got a gripe, and he's had a go at the Commanding Officer with a knife. But we let it go.' I said: 'Oh? Really! Oh, good. Oh, super.' So I sat next to this brooding guy and I started chatting to him, saying: 'I hear you've had a bit of bad luck.' It turned out that the real agony was that his girlfriend had left him. He showed me a picture of an awful old stripper from some club, who'd obviously slept with half the bloody army. Anyway, I soothed him down and was doing very well.

But then the mates I'd made in the NAAFI came rolling round and said: 'Come and have a drink in our hut.' So I was suddenly plucked away from all these blokes in my own billet, and I was sitting up in the Regulars' hut, getting pissed out of my mind with them, and hearing the most amazing stories about one of the sergeants' wives that they'd all been laying while he was off on active service. I staggered back to my hut and was promptly the following morning put in charge of it. The bloke said: 'You look a responsible man. You are responsible for the hut and the cleanliness of the hut, and you see these lads get on with their work. And you will be responsible for checking in the coal quota – and, by the way, some of the coal quota comes to me. You do that, and I'll see you're all right.' So I said: 'Oh. Yes.' I was into a whole racket, immediately! I was beginning to quite enjoy it. We were marched across to the medical orderly. Fortunately, I chose Door 3. Door 2 was a cantankerous old bugger: any man who could crawl in there was immediately sent in – very good for them. Door 3 was a National Service Officer, a medic, who was actually writing a book about his experiences as a National Service Medical Officer, brief as they were. So we got on to literature, and he found I was a writer, which I played up a little when I discovered that was his leaning, too. I also claimed to have an agent, which I did have at that time, just, and said I could probably see him right for his book. To which he said: 'Do you want to do this?' To which I said: 'Not a bit.' He said: 'No, I didn't think you looked too keen.' He said. 'But how do we get you out? You seem to be perfectly fit. Ah! Ah! A knee, a knee. What's this knee?' And I said: 'Well, it's cricket knee; I twisted it when I was young. I tried it on when I went for my medical in Leicester; they weren't prepared to buy it, but they did put it down as suspect.' He said: 'Well, it's graded "quite safe" at the moment, but, having had another look at it,' he said, 'I don't like the look of that at all. How far could you walk on that knee, if you were asked?' I said: 'Well, probably about as far as from here to the NAAFI *safely*, but not a lot further.' He said: 'Could it give?' I said: 'It would probably give.' He said: 'And if it did give, do you realise what you'd be doing?' I said: 'No.' He said: 'You'd be invalided out of the RAF and we'd have to pay you a very large pension for the rest of your life. At nineteen years old, I don't think that is a responsible thing for me to do. So, all I can say is: get out, you're the sort of man we don't want!' So I staggered out of the hut with my pink chit, while the guy next door, who'd got a perforated eardrum, was hurled out by this nasty old bloke who'd said: 'You're perfectly fit!'

It's very hard to get out of the RAF, or any service. It's easy enough to get in: you see one man. To get you out you have to see fifteen, all of whom countersign your chit, any of whom at any moment, you feel, is going to say: 'Just a minute!' I got to the very last man at five o'clock that day; and he said: 'Closed!' I said: 'It's just to sign . . . ' He said: 'Tomorrow morning! My office is open at nine. Not until then. Goodnight!' I thought: 'Hell! Another night: anything can happen.' I went to the pictures, and had an extreme amount to drink with my Regular friends again. I was actually getting delirious. They liked the fact that I was in show business, but they weren't too sure about just being in theatre. So I invented: I was a great friend of Cliff Michelmore, I remember. They said: 'Do you actually know him?' I said: 'Oh yes, yes indeed. Cliff and I have drinks together. And I write for television'. The following morning I rushed through the gates of the camp, past two suspicious armed guards, waving my exit visa — my promise that, if the war broke out, I would not be recalled, except as a sort of strategic, non-active combatant. 'Wait for the bus,' they said. 'No.' I said. 'I'm walking,' and I ran to the station, phoned my wife and was home that day.

Oddly enough, I then phoned Stephen, because he'd tried to get me out. He'd written a long letter saying: 'The whole future of the English theatre depends on this man.' It hadn't had much effect with the army. 'Ah!' he said, 'I'm glad you phoned, because our electrician has just walked out. If you come to Newcastle, I'm lighting the show tomorrow afternoon. You know what I'm like with ladders; if you're there, I really will appreciate it.' I said: 'Stephen, there's no problem. I'll be there in the afternoon. Don't worry.' So, saying a brief farewell, I got on the train and went to Newcastle-on-Tyne. Getting back to Newcastle-under-Lyme took a long time! I arrived at seven, and ran up the Municipal Hall steps, and saw him at the top. I said: 'Stephen, I'm sorry. Did you manage to light it?' He'd got his whole arm in plaster, and he said: 'No, I didn't. I fell off the ladder.' I said: 'Oh Christ! I'm so sorry. I mean, it was the train, and I . . . ' He said: 'I not only fell off the ladder, I fell on to the office.' From the description later, how he hadn't killed himself, I don't know. He'd fallen off a high ladder, off one of his own gantry things. He'd landed on top of the table which was, in fact, the office. He'd completely crushed the portable typewriter to death – it was just flat. And all the money and everything had gone flying. Anyway, I was back in theatre!

IW   And *Love After All* was in the repertoire at the time. That was a costume farce.

AA   Yes. I didn't write it in any particular period, because I wasn't that clever, but it was obviously going to be a period thing, because it was based on *The Barber of Seville*. I remember seeing the play at school. The suitor keeps coming back and disguising himself, getting in as a music teacher. I tinkered around with it a lot. And in the first version, with Clifford Williams directing, it was a very good production – it was very tight and quite fun, and we did it Edwardian. It was later revived, the following summer I think, with me playing the lead; and it was directed by Julian Herrington, who decided there were certain bits of it he didn't like very much, like its Edwardianness, and its rather jokey names. He brought it up to date, and I don't think the play actually gained from what we did to it. And the third play followed very hotly on that.

IW   Which was *Dad's Tale*.

AA   Which again Clifford came back to direct. And it was not a success. It was not a success *(a)* because I think we were into a winter season in Scarborough, which never established itself; and *(b)* because it was a children's play. It was certainly more successful than my second children's play, but we were actually doing it at a time when there weren't any children around! Instead of doing it in school time, when you could con a few of them in there, we were doing it just before Christmas. And it had a disastrous first night.

It had an extraordinary brief. It was written for two companies, us and the British Dance Drama Theatre, who weren't going to meet until very late on in rehearsals. Clifford was directing our company; Gerard Bagley was directing the dance company. And what I had to do was write the play overall, then write separately the story that the ballet should take. They were to rehearse this entirely separately, and then we fused them together when the two companies got together in Scarborough; in fact, once or twice the actors got involved in the ballets; but they were always pushed around or shoved into places. It was quite an adventurous show, really.

IW   Was it funny?

AA   It was meant to be. I think it was. It never actually got an audience to prove it.

IW   Your second children's play was *Christmas v Mastermind* – that was the real disaster.

AA   That was the most disastrous play I've ever done. It was the only one of mine that Peter Cheeseman directed and I think we had very different views on what children's theatre should be about. Peter and I have actually grown together a lot more in recent years. At that time, I think we were diametrically opposed about many things.

We had some quite good arguments, and I was his associate director, so it was quite a merry time. But I suppose if you're living together for eighteen months, in those conditions, it's natural you're going to have big rows. Certainly, that play was one that he shouldn't have done. I probably shouldn't have written it either, but it had pieces of whimsy in it which we might just have brought off. It was the first winter in Stoke, so there was again no audience. It's lovely to see now that the theatre is pre-sold ten weeks, or something, but at that time we got no audiences at all. It was a play about Father Christmas, who was actually a very unpleasant old man. He was faced with industrial trouble. His chief gnome had called the men out. The gnome was inspired by an evil character called the Crimson Golliwog, who was not that at all, but who had a special gang whose object was to take over Father Christmas anyway. They incited the gnome to this revolutionary action just before Christmas and also abducted his fairy helper. It was quite a broad, jolly farce, with lots of fights in telephone boxes. And there were two policeman, who tracked everything down, disguised as hedges and letterboxes. But it was received in dreadful silence. None of it seemed to succeed and we died the death with it.

IW   All these plays we've been talking about are plays which you would rather forget in many ways, wouldn't you?

Christmas v. Mastermind at Stoke: Alan Ayckbourn with Elizabeth Bell, David Wehner and Peter King

AA I think you've got to be allowed a certain amount of learning time – you know, learning what you can do as well as learning what you can't do, really; and I think in *Christmas v Mastermind* I was learning what I can't do. I can't write successfully for kids, because I don't have the interest. And all the best children's writers I've met have been totally devoted to what they're doing.

IW But you later came up with *Ernie's Incredible Illucinations*, which got published and which is rather sweet.

AA Yes, it does a tremendous number of performances. That is the exception. And I've had endless letters to write a sequel, which I've always resisted, because I think I could not actually do it very well. I said: 'The whole point of the script is that you write your own sequel. The thing is a starting point for imaginative games. And if you want to do *Ernie Goes to the Moon*, you do it.'

IW But the first plays, the ones right from the beginning: you never allow them to be done?

AA No. With all the best will in the world, however keen one was on my work, I don't think anyone would want to revive them.

TO THE WEST END – AND BROADWAY

IW   You talked about *Standing Room Only* to the extent of saying that its provenance was one of Stephen's current fads, which was the population problem. He wanted to set it on Venus and you couldn't quite get it together with Venus! *Standing Room Only* is set in the ultimate traffic jam, in a bus on Shaftesbury Avenue. And, as you said before, the play is actually about a whole lot of personal relationships rather than about the traffic jam. Peter Bridge bought an option on this for town, didn't he?

AA   Yes, it was the first play I sold to him.

IW   It looked very much as if it was going to get into town at one stage. I believe he even bought a bus to set it in, didn't he?

AA   Yes, he did, I think. It was the most re-written play ever.

IW   Now why was that? In its Scarborough version it was very simple, a very small cast play. I've read three different versions of it, with god knows how many people in the cast: was this all Peter Bridge's influence, that it had to be re-written?

AA   Yes. It was written in Scarborough originally, and it was a nice, simple little piece. The reason it ever attracted attention – which may be the whole source of my being a successful dramatist – was that *The Stage* critic at Scarborough was unable to attend the show; and *The Stage* at that time were not averse to asking someone in a management to write their own notice. Joan Macalpine actually wrote the review, and she was the acting manager of the theatre. And she wrote a corker, because, well, who wouldn't? And she wrote, in an inspired burst: 'Will no management drive this bus into Shaftesbury Avenue?' This appeared dutifully in *The Stage*, on the rep page; at which point Peter Bridge, in his office, swivelled in his chair, thought: 'Good lord, this is a must!' and rushed to Scarborough, introduced himself and took out an option. He was very impressive, promised – as Peter was wont to do – that this would be the biggy, but explained to me quite carefully that the West End was necessarily a star system. And Peter Bridge was particularly noted, of course, for mounting shows which were very, very star-studded. Most of his productions were revivals.
   Then began the bizarre history of this play, when he offered it to one star and then

Stephen Joseph directing *Standing Room Only*

another. And I suppose it was typical of my plays in that it didn't really have star parts: it had quite a good part for the father and a couple of reasonable parts for the girls, but none of the parts was particularly *per se* what you would call a star part. So what happened was he sent it round; Richard Wattis had it, Hattie Jacques had it, Sidney James had it and Ron Moody had it – all sorts. I think about fifteen or twenty stars had it eventually, all of whom were up for different parts. So, on each occasion, Peter would give me a quick ring and say: 'Look, I'm sending this to X. I've put him up for John. I think the part doesn't look so good: could you build it up a little? And he's six-foot-two, with glasses and thinning hair and a wart on his chin: I wonder if you could just build that description into the character?' So I'd write: '*Enter John, a bespectacled man of six-foot-two, thinning hair, with a wart on his chin,*' you see.

And so this would go off for a start. He could hardly have been fooled by this artifice into presuming it was a coincidence. Anyway, they would then add their four-penn'orth. I remember meeting the late Sid James, who said: 'It's a very good script. Very nice script, son.' He said: 'I'll tell you what's wrong with it.' I said: 'Oh yes?' He said: 'It wants a few more rudes in it.' I said: 'I beg your pardon?' He said: 'Rudes. It's a very clean script. You know, I mean, a few bloodies and things, just to liven it up.' I said: 'Oh. Thank you very much.' I didn't say I thought I'd achieved something monumentally clever by actually avoiding this! So off I went.

I got a bit angry eventually. And indeed, the script began to get more and more misshapen, as every single part was built up. In fact, at one point, when Sid James was in contention as the bus driver – he was at that time doing a television series with Sydney Tafler – I was encouraged to write a second bus driver in, called Bert or something, in order to cater for Sydney Tafler, who I don't think actually got to read the script anyway. I would have finished up writing the entire *Carry On* crew eventually! So the play, from its slender Scarborough beginnings, became really very complex and unmanageable and unwieldy. And I suppose, over two years, I must have re-written it again and again and again, till I had helicopters flying in.

IW   Yes, the ending changed quite remarkably. I seem to remember at Scarborough it ended up with the joyous cry of: 'We're moving! We're moving!' Then I suddenly came to read a script, and you've got helicopter cranes lifting the whole bloody lot up.

AA   That was the West End version, which was never done and never could have been done. They said: 'We want something a bit more spectacular!' And at that time, Peter was putting on *Come Spy With Me* with Danny La Rue, who was flown in in a helicopter; and he said this would make a good ending. And obviously a dramatist of that experience and that age – and one looks back on oneself with horror: the unprotected boy! – was open to suggestions from the office cleaner onwards. Everybody wanted to get in on the act. I suppose there's a reaction now: I'm very wary about any suggestion from anyone, except people I trust very much. Eventually we did the play again at Stoke, in a modified version from Scarborough. I think it was quite a good show.

IW   Did Peter Bridge eventually drop it, or did you drop him?

AA   It never came off. It just went on and on and on, until I suppose everyone had tried to do it. He still tried – I gave up. I said: 'I'm absolutely exhausted. I cannot continue. I've been through three different directors, all of whom said: "Yes, I like it. I think this is what we want to do." I've gone and stayed at their houses, and . . . '

IW   Who were they?

Mr. Whatnot at Stoke

AA   John Hale was one, in Bristol. There was an Irishman called Jim Fitzgerald. Oh, and I met Bob Chetwyn, I think. I met a lot of people: I went round the directors. But eventually I did the play again in Stoke, as I say, and that was that. I exorcised it.

IW   *Mr Whatnot* was the one which Peter Bridge did actually get into town.

AA   He was a stayer, Bridge. He came back for more. After that, many a management would have turned their back.

IW   *Mr Whatnot* was written for Stoke-on-Trent. Did you direct it there yourself?

AA   Yes. After reviving *Standing Room Only* at Stoke I wrote *Mr Whatnot* – which is actually the second original play I wrote for Stoke, after *Christmas v Mastermind*.

IW   What was the basis of *Mr Whatnot*? Was it the actors you had in the company at Stoke? Or was it a hankering after a mime play?

AA   Several factors all came together. We had an actor, Peter King, in his first season, who had a natural ability for mime: he was a very clean, clear, in fact a very strong mime actor,

Alan Ayckbourn's last acting role, in William Gibson's *Two for the Seesaw* with Heather Stoney

and I always thought that it would be nice to use him more in that context. Secondly, I've got a great fondness for silent film, all the old classics – particularly the Buster Keatons and the Harold Lloyds and people like that, rather more than Chaplin. I'd also seen a couple of films by René Clair, particularly *Le Million*, which I was terribly taken with, and which had wondrous sequences. A mackintosh becomes a rugby ball: he would take a sequence, elaborate it, and transform it into another sequence about something quite different, with just a wave of the hand and a sound effect. I rather like that. And *Whatnot* started by using common jargon from other media and transposing it into a theatre setting, something I've done quite a lot – things like the car chase and running across ploughed fields in the morning, and a lot of filmic sequences of lovers in the sunset, and operas, and people dining in restaurants with gipsy violinists. It was firstly based around Peter himself, as the actor: he was very much in my mind when I wrote it. I was also aware that we had (you can't not be aware after working with them for so long) a group of actors who would perhaps be very responsive to this. It was, significantly, the first play I wrote for myself as a director. It was when I was going through my 'If-I-can't-show-myself-off-as-an-actor-I'll-show-myself-off-as-a-director' phase.

IW You weren't in it?

AA I wasn't in it. It was the first one I wasn't in, which is also significant. And it was also significantly, in retrospect, my most successful play to date. It became a very, very successful production, in its Stoke form, and was the first original, major smash we had there. It pre-dated, of course, subsequent big hits like *The Knotty*, which Peter Cheeseman went on to do when he developed the house style.

IW It's based on a really quite remarkable suspension of disbelief, because Mint is not actually dumb, is he?

AA He just can't think of anything to say!

IW But he's played mute throughout. Even in his telephone conversations, he doesn't say anything.

AA Yes, I originally wanted to write it with no dialogue at all. And, in fact, when I wrote the dialogue, I asked the actors to learn it and then distort it; so that: 'Jolly nice day!' would become: 'Wah-wah wah wah!' and so on. However, when they were playing the dialogue, it actually was quite funny, and they were rather reluctant to let some of it go. So, in the end, not altogether sorry, I conceded that they could keep the dialogue that was there. Yes, it was interesting to have a totally silent hero. My instructions to the actor were that they shouldn't really notice he hadn't spoken. I didn't want to make a great issue of him being a silent man, but it seemed to me that silence in a character creates a richness of its own. I mean, I would be crestfallen had I ever heard Buster Keaton speak, let's put it that way. It's rather like seeing your favourite radio actor in the flesh. We all know what Dick Barton looked like. I never wanted to meet him, because he wouldn't have the right eyebrows, the right square shoulders. He was totally in the eye of the listener. And in the same way, the sound, and a lot of the personality, of a silent actor was in the eye of the watcher. And indeed, I've seen a great variety in the Whatnots over the years. Paul Moriarty played him: it was a wonderful performance, he was a very good Whatnot. But it was a totally different, more dangerous, manic Whatnot that he played. Peter King is Welsh – he was a Welsh Whatnot; they're very rapacious and his was a very sexy Whatnot.

IW How can he be a Welsh Whatnot if he's totally silent?

AA Ah, he had Welsh looks and he had that dark, Celtic lust. He was very lustful. The thing that the successful productions did, and that the London production did not do, was to remain always fairly salacious. There was a danger that Amanda was going to get some horrific come-uppance when she did get into bed with Whatnot, because he would stop at nothing. And that was the nice thing about it – he didn't have a romantic image of her at all, he wanted her body: and as long as that happened, it gave the play a sort of balls, I think, which it totally lacked when he wanted to give her a flower. Cecil wanted to give her flowers and chocolates: Whatnot wanted to give her what-for! And indeed, one has suggested that this is all she was really wanting as well: she was certainly looking around hoping that something was going to happen. And in that sense our heroes both had their feet on the ground.

IW When it's produced, presumably it can run anything from about fifty minutes to two hours.

AA Yes, it's very flexible. What I've always said is that the script is there as a basis. In fact, the basis is very workable and one should beware of throwing things out or over-embroidering. Certainly there's a greater danger of over-embroidering than of throwing things out. But it is best, I think, played when the subordinate parts are kept very well set and the things like the tennis sequence are highly rehearsed, and allow set cadenzas for the Whatnot. If you've got a Whatnot who does handstands, it's useful to put them in somewhere. Peter was extremely nimble and obviously his Whatnot had more than a great fear of dogs, and it was nice to use that side of him. I've seen more ferocious and large Whatnots being able to cope with the dog better, and had to find other ways round it.

IW Peter King went to London with it, didn't he? What went wrong with the London production?

AA Oh lord, almost everything went wrong with the London production. Peter Bridge bought it. He first of all suggested we take the whole production down. Peter Cheeseman was less than enthusiastic about taking the whole cast, but agreed. But Peter Bridge then went back on that and said: 'No, perhaps this is a bit risky. Perhaps we should think about getting a slightly better-known cast. And perhaps, on second thoughts, the director shouldn't also be the writer, because writer-directors are not a good idea.' So, could I think of anybody? And I said: 'Well, yes, why not Clifford Williams?' because he, after all, had done two of my earlier shows and I liked him. Clifford came up: he was at the Royal Shakespeare Company by then. He was heavily involved, I think quite liked the show but said he couldn't do it himself, and suggested another Welshman – Welshmen stick together, you see – Warren Jenkins. Warren I didn't know, but he was then directing at Cardiff.

Where it didn't work, to put it bluntly, was that he was not happy with the play and he was not happy with the company, which I think was the most extraordinary mixture of talents. There was a young Judy Cornwell, there was a youngish Ronnie Barker, as headstrong as Ronnie is now, a very talented Ronnie Stevens, who also wanted to go his own way; and Judy Campbell, who was a totally straight actress, and Diane Clare, totally straight – both in their way experienced. And then, in the middle of this, a very young actor straight from the provinces, thrown in as the lead, who was to dominate the whole thing: and a very young Chris Godwin also, playing the vicar and the pedestrian. The other member of the cast was Marie Lohr, a wonderful old lady who was actually the right age to play it – well, strictly she was too old to play it, she was in her seventies – and she gamely battled through the script, playing vigorous games of imaginary tennis, and broke her knee. So she was labouring under the most terrible handicap by the time we opened, with her knee strapped up. Anyway, that was the chemistry. That was the first thing: that the balance of cast and the director itself was wrong. The second thing that was wrong was that it was over-produced, and that far too much money was spent on it. Peter Rice, who'd done a lot of very nice designs for operas, came in and did some very, very decorative sets, none of which added to it. He added slides to a show that supposedly had to do with imagination.

The other thing I learnt was that whilst theatre in the round can be quite small, every square inch of space is viable playing space; when you put something on to an equivalent quite small pros stage, there is no way you can get it all on. Warren had put in some very charming music by Vivian Ellis, which was totally wrong. I was looking for Ibert and Poulenc – those very French things. I wanted spiky little French tunes, and I was getting rather nice little English tunes. And the thing was rapidly becoming very chintzy and very charming. It was in fact, as I think one critic called it, a very gushy evening, very pretty, very winsome. I find Marcel Marceau slightly charming, but he opened the same week as us (which wasn't a very good omen), and by comparison his show was so butch it was unbelievable. We were fairytime, you know. If ever a show deserved to close, that one did.

IW   Were you able to rationalise it that way at the time? Were you sufficiently objective to do that?

Judy Campbell, Ronnie Barker and Marie Lohr in the London production of *Mr. Whatnot*

AA When a show goes wrong, it all goes wrong. I had actors coming and saying: 'You must get rid of this director.' We had emotional storms: the leading lady collapsed and cried all over me at the dress rehearsal. She was in a terrible state. Everything was dissolving and tensions were mounting.

IW How old were you at this time?

AA I was too young for that to happen. I was in my early twenties.

IW Was Peter Bridge supportive?

AA Like most producers, Peter wasn't able to help much in such a situation. He came in and made a few general suggestions for new jokes. But what we didn't want was new jokes: we wanted the old ones to be got right. I think the basic thing wrong was the ingredients; if you get the wrong ingredients, you can stir them round all you like, and shake them, but it isn't going to work. However, good things came of it.

IW *Futtocks End*, the television film, grew out of it, didn't it?

AA *Futtocks End*? Well, yes, but that was nothing to do with me. That was Ronnie Barker's. The best thing that came of *Whatnot* was that Michael Hordern's wife saw it and liked it; and some years later when Peter Bridge sent a script of *Relatively Speaking* to Michael to consider, his wife said: 'Oh, if it's by that man who wrote that play, it'll be wonderful. Do read it.' And it certainly helped in the cause. And a lot of people saw *Whatnot* who subsequently felt they really had jumped on it rather hard, and I've been lucky enough to get a sort of guilt vote back again.

IW You revived it for the opening at Scarborough of what is now the Stephen Joseph Theatre. Is it due for any more revivals ever?

AA No. I don't know that I should revive my plays. I think other people should do that.

IW You gave up your job at Stoke to see the play into town, didn't you?

AA Everyone had convinced me that this was going to be the big one. Again, young days. What one tries to say to writers is: wait.

IW Yes. Why on earth had you given up your job, because you weren't directing the show, you weren't in the show in town?

Alan Ayckbourn with Peter Cheeseman, director of the Victoria Theatre, Stoke-on-Trent

AA   There were other reasons for leaving Stoke, although this provided a spur. The theatre was not able to contain both Peter Cheeseman and me. I was co-directing alongside him. I had been directing long before he joined – I'd probably been directing long before he started directing. And it was difficult for him to work with an associate director who in fact had introduced him to the round. And, as he developed – and he developed very fast – he got very strong ideas about what he wanted to do with that theatre, which didn't necessarily coincide with mine. The rift with Stephen didn't help, because he always felt, at that point (he certainly doesn't now) that I was a Stephen man and not a Cheeseman man.

IW   Surely the rift with Stephen didn't come until sometime later.

AA   It was there early. Stephen asked me over to Scarborough one weekend from Stoke, and said to me: 'I want you to take over the theatre. I'm going to get rid of Peter.' And I said 'I don't think I can do that.' It's something I've always been rather proud I said, because it was something I would love to have done, but I said: 'No, I don't think I can do that,

Stephen, because I would actually lose all the people I'm working with.' It would have been such an act of awfulness, to have gone back and just ousted Peter – apart from the fact that I actually liked Peter very much and I did respect him, although I argued with him furiously about the round. But Stephen was obviously extremely frustrated and angry.

IW   What sort of arguments were you having with Peter? You say you argued with him incessantly about the round: was this ideological?

AA   Yes, mainly. Peter was much more of an academic director and I, as it were, had risen through the ranks to direct. And I suppose it had something to do with my position as an actor/director. I was still in that peculiar position of acting in every other production, playing the lead more often than not, and then directing the next one. Peter didn't have that proximity. He just came in and directed every other play. Our main argument revolved around the fact that Peter believed essentially (and this is to put it a bit crudely) that no actor could do anything unless he fully understood the concept. That is to say, no actor could play a nuclear scientist unless he had read all the books about nuclear science. I said: 'No, that's not true: the most stupid actors can often play brilliant nuclear scientists. If the script is good, they convince you; and it isn't necessary always to break everything down and examine it to that extent, and iron out what is the truth.' And Stan Page and I, who were the two older-stagers, at the raw ages of about twenty-three and thirty, both insisted that there was such a thing as an actor's instinct, which must be allowed to flourish. Peter denied it, very strongly at that point, and said: 'No. If it isn't intellectually acceptable, then it can't be done emotionally.' And I suppose we shouted a lot about this.

   Most of my work was done on the assumption that actors got there by instinct. Indeed, we had a boy in the company at that time – Peter King in fact – who worked entirely on instinct. He was, I think he would say himself, an extremely unschooled Welshman, who has since schooled himself enormously and read copiously and become really quite erudite. At that point, though, he could hardly join his letters together, and yet he remained a very fine instinctive actor. I think probably, in fact, his learning damned him as an actor. There is an old saying that a few coarse directors use: 'Give me a stupid actor and you'll find a good one.' And indeed, actors can be too clever for their own good. But Peter was a standing example of a man who could play anything. He could play Prime Minister, with a gravity and solemnity and authority, and apparent knowledge of politics which, of course, he didn't really have: he just had the script.

IW   How did Peter Cheeseman take this? Presumably he could see that Peter King could act?

AA   Yes, but he would say: 'Well, it's not true, because he doesn't. We know.' And I'd say: 'Well no, but nobody else knows.' I suppose we were a little bit more show-biz than Peter. He was graduating rapidly towards the documentary, at that point, where he found it dramatic for real shop stewards to stand up and tell you about their day-to-day plight; which became dramatic because they were real shop stewards. I was moving rapidly in another direction.

IW   He was also moving towards the integration of actors into the community as ordinary members who ought to share the concerns of the community, wasn't he?

AA   Oh sure. It was the beginning of a very interesting rift. Are actors as other men, or are they not? I don't know. The public, I suspect, prefer them not to be.

IW   They'd rather have them glamorous, you mean?

AA   Yes. I run a theatre where the actors go and drink in the bar, but I'm sure that most of the public would love them to jump into the Rolls and steam off. They're all in variety now, those sorts of stars. There still are a few in Scarborough, and they're the people that the public is really fascinated by – when Danny La Rue arrives, there's a sort of air of glamour about. I think I believe a bit more in the illusion of theatre than Peter did, though he's come round to that more now. At that point we were poles apart: I think we're actually quite close now.

IW   Anyway, it was enough to push you out of the theatre.

AA   It was time to go. We all decided to go. New people were coming in, the old order was changing, you know. We were getting a bit dinosaur-like, really.

IW   So, you went to town, and you took this great critical drubbing. How – it's a daft question, but how hard did you actually take that critical reaction to *Mr Whatnot*?

AA   I took it very hard, actually. I was very, very upset; although I was cushioned by the fact that I sort of knew it was going to happen. But it was enough to stop me writing for quite a long time. I gave up. I joined the BBC with no thought of writing again – certainly not for London or the stage.

IW   How did the radio job come about?

AA   Oh, that was funny. Everything happens by odd coincidences. I'd got an agent, of course, Peggy Ramsay, and I rang her a couple of days after *Whatnot* had opened, just for commiseration. Peggy is great on commiseration: she can bolster you up in no time. By chance, in the office was another client of hers at that time, Alfred Bradley (Senior Drama Producer for BBC North Region Radio), who was writing children's work mainly. He realised that his half-an-hour in London with Peggy was going to be absolutely wiped out if he allowed me to stay on the phone to her, because I needed half an hour at least with Peggy, while she told me that the critics were all bastards, and all that. So Alfred said: 'Get him off the phone. Tell him to write for the job.'

IW   You must have known Alfred at this time.

AA   Oh, I did, yes. Alfred I'd known because he'd come over and seen quite a few productions – mostly at Scarborough, some at Stoke. He was a friend of Stephen's. He said: 'Get him off the line. Tell him to apply for the job.' Peggy said: 'Alf's here.' I said: 'Alf who?' She said: 'Alf Bradley.' I said: 'Oh yes? Great.' She said: 'He says apply for the job in the *New Statesman*. Get a last week's *New Statesman*, and there's a good job in it, and he says you could stand a good chance if you apply.' And I said: 'Well, I . . .' 'Cheerio, now!' said Peggy, and bang! Down went the phone. So I waited a few days, and then I thought: 'Oh well!' So I dug out an old *New Statesman*, and there was this job, so I wrote off. The BBC took ages and then they sent me an application form, and I wrote back again. And then I got the board. I travelled up to Leeds, got seen by this committee, and Alfred was very encouraging. I realised that they would interview the candidates and, provided they looked as if they weren't going to blow the building up, they would then ask Alfred which one he liked. At that point, I think I was probably the one with the most active directing experience; so he said to me: 'Well, unless Tyrone Guthrie applies, I think you're OK on the present showing.' Nicely the job did come my way with an astronomic salary. It was £38 a week: it was unbelievable.

IW   What were you being paid in the theatre at this time?

AA   Funnily enough, the highest I got to was in my swansong week as an actor at Rotherham, on £18. But at Stoke it was about £12.

IW   You stayed in the BBC for six years, but during that time Stephen Joseph coaxed you back into the theatre, didn't he, first as a writer and then as a director?

AA   Yes, Stephen asked me for a play for the 1965 summer season in Scarborough, and I did my well-made-play bit.

IW   That was *Meet My Father*, which, once again, Peter Bridge picked up for town. This

Richard Briers and Celia Johnson in the West End production of *Relatively Speaking*

time, though, he gave it a new title, *Relatively Speaking*, a cast with a chemistry which clearly worked wonderfully well – in Celia Johnson, Michael Hordern, Richard Briers and Jennifer Hilary – and it was a runaway success in the West End. I think a lot of people at that stage probably heaved a sigh of relief and said: 'Thank god! Ayckbourn's hit the winning formula at last.' Noel Coward sent you a telegram of congratulation after seeing the show, and you were clearly being groomed to assume his mantle. But your next show for Scarborough – to which Peter Bridge and Nigel Patrick (who had directed *Relatively*) came running – was *The Sparrow*, a straight chronological narrative, devoid of deft plot manipulation, about four distinctly unglamorous young people in a grotty flat. I suppose, in retrospect, it was the first of your more sour examinations of the state of marriage. It played to full houses during the summer in Scarborough, but I vividly remember – because I worked as Stage Director on the production – the brittle smile on Nigel Patrick's face as he greeted the actors after the show. 'Many congratulations!' he said to each of them in turn, and then moved grimly on as quickly as he could. He obviously couldn't get back to town fast enough! The show never made the West End.

AA   No. I don't believe, in retrospect, that it's as good a play as *Relatively*, but it's only had three weeks in its life, those three weeks at Scarborough. It's probably worth a little more than that. At the time, the only reason it was suppressed was that somebody said it was a bit like *The Knack*. Since I hadn't seen *The Knack*, I didn't realise. I've seen *The Knack* since. It *is* a bit like *The Knack* – it's got a girl in the lead, that's what it was. But then, so has *Antony and Cleopatra*.

IW   And then came *How The Other Half Loves*, which got star-parted with Robert Morley and ran for ages. What did Morley do to it?

AA   Well, he started honestly enough: he did play it down the middle. He's an actor who rapidly gets very bored, and in order to refresh himself and to engage himself he always treats the theatre as one huge game organised by himself. The joy of the man is that he does have great enjoyment for what he does, an infectious, playful enthusiasm. Unfortunately, the people who suffer are the people who are on stage with him, or who are attempting to get on stage with him. And there's a few working actors ploughing doggedly through their script, clutching on to their characterisation, which he almost delights in bombarding and trying to upset – hiding their props and locking the door and jumping out at them from cupboards. Which is all right but it tends to make them look awfully ropey. It also tends to make the play look a little bit ropey. In the case of *How The Other Half*, he tended to improvise round the theme quite a lot, but – because it was such a complex plot – he was unable to do perhaps as much as he would like to have done with it. I believe people like Peter Ustinov have rather stronger views about what he did to *Halfway Up A Tree*, but with *How The Other Half*, I didn't actually go to see it after a bit, because there was no point in getting unnecessarily upset. I was a younger, more vulnerable author then. The night I did see it, I was terribly upset, because nothing seemed to be as we had originally arranged it.

IW   Did you clash with him personally?

AA   I would have done if I'd been stronger and had the nerve. I would do now, certainly. At that point, I was a very new author with a very new play, and I tended to sit rather quietly and weep in corners. But certainly the director, Robin Midgley, clashed with him on notable occasions before we opened – not necessarily with Robert, but with what Robert wanted. The trouble with Robert's area of interest is that it doesn't stop at his own performance. He was very insistent that, for instance, his leading lady should play it this way, and that somebody else should play it that way. He is in a sense an actor-manager. He wanted all the parts played as he wanted to play it. Now that wasn't necessarily the way that Robin wanted them or I wanted them. Fiona, in *How The Other Half*, is really a quite vicious character: she's not as vicious as some of her later versions, but she's an unfaithful wife who deceives her husband and plays a very sly game. Robert wouldn't have any of that. Her attitude to her husband up to the end was one of crushing and withering sarcasm a lot of the time. Robert insisted that anyone who was on stage with him should look as if they loved him; so, luckless Joan Tetzel and more luckless Jan Holden were forced to play against what the character was actually doing. I remember him quite vehemently saying: 'Look, nobody wants to come to the theatre and see people squabbling' – which dismissed about three-quarters of English drama, I should have thought. But he said: 'We don't want all these nasty cross people, and people shouting at each other.' A lot of *How The Other Half Loves* is about people getting extremely angry with each other; and when you get into the realms of Bob and Terry, whose whole relationship is teetering on the edge of disaster, and you start laying down the law and saying: 'No, you must love each other', then you aren't left with a lot of the mainspring of the play. In that sense the quarrel was there; but as to his performance, he turned in a lovely performance of Frank. If he'd actually had the courage to stick to the script – or perhaps the

Robert Morley with Heather Sears and Jan Holden
in the West End production of *How the Other Half Loves*

faith to stick to the script – a little bit more closely, it could have been an even better one. But I learned one great maxim from Robert, and that was that you can't argue with the system. Eighty per cent of that audience had paid to see Robert Morley, and I, as an unknown dramatist, had really no right to stand between that process if I wanted to take the money. If I could have suffocated Robert to the extent of preventing him from doing his own thing, I think I would have actually offended many punters. They would have walked away awfully offended.

How the Other Half Loves at Scarborough

IW   Though it needs to be said that by this time you were already through *Relatively Speaking*, which had been a tremendous success.

AA   Well, it was only my second. But the lesson itself was learnt even more vigorously and vividly with *Me Times Me* when Celia Johnson toured it, with Roland Culver. Celia was, quite naturally, the star of the evening and had, rather against her better judgement, accepted the part due to the soft-forked tongue of Michael Codron, who had promised her the moon if she came into it. And she'd agreed, with fond memories, I think, of *Relatively*, which was a great performance by her. The part was considerably smaller, the stage time that she occupied was quite small. We took it on a tour, which included Brighton. In Brighton, again eighty per cent of the audience came to see Celia Johnson. But they didn't see Celia Johnson: they saw seven or eight other actors, with occasional appearances by Celia Johnson; and you could feel the temperature drop in that theatre when she went off.

They said: 'Oh, this can't be an important scene because the star isn't on.' And I learned very quickly that, if you're going to have a star, it's got to be in a star part. There's actually quite a damaging thing in trying to persuade a star to play a part that isn't a star part. It seems quite an obvious truism, but you have to learn it the hard way.

IW   Yes, once again, *Me Times Me* never made it to the West End, despite going out on tour twice – though Sam Walters revived it as *Family Circles* at the Orange Tree in Richmond in 1978. You don't write star parts; you said that before.

AA   No.

IW   And really, *How The Other Half Loves* was rehabilitated by the Actors Company, wasn't it?

AA   Yes, it was quite recently with Moray Watson, Barbara Murray, Stephanie Turner and Simon Cadell. It was very good; it was done by the right people. In fact, it restored the play. A lot of critics re-reviewed it – or critics who weren't around when it was first done, including people like Levin, I think, and Cushman, certainly – and it got nice notices; and it was very nice to see the old play restored. One of the most extraordinary things about the whole West End experience, the first time around, was that whilst it contained elaborately sophisticated time shifts, and was an extraordinary piece of staging – with that super-imposed stage – not a single critic, to my knowledge, ever mentioned it. So something had got blurred! It's not normal, I'd have thought – it certainly wasn't normal in our time – for people to do English light comedy with superimposed time scales; and at one point, there were three sets of people on stage, two of them living at different time levels and one pair living at both time levels. It really is quite complicated, and nobody even mentioned it.

IW   *How The Other Half* introduced you to Broadway, didn't it?

AA   Yes. It was an experiment: *Relatively* had never come off in America, because I'd quarrelled vigorously with their attempts to Americanise it. In this one, I did meet a marvellous man called Gene Saks who was directing it, and with whom I hit it off immedi-ately; and we sat down, and with his advice I Americanised the script myself. It didn't help the play, in retrospect. At the time it was a very painless way to do it, because he just said: 'We would say that round the other way.' And as we did it, slowly we began to thin the language out and narrow down the subtleties. Sometimes he would add something very useful, but he was not a writer, he was a director, and I was not fluent in American. So the version was an unhappy compromise in many ways, although it worked, up to a point. The plot was the strong thing, and the machinations of that; and that certainly worked. We had a

How the Other Half Loves at the Riksteatern, Solna, Sweden

very good cast. It had a good tour, but it rose and fell really on its first night on Broadway, and it didn't pass the post. It got a lukewarm review from Clive Barnes, who at that point was the be-all-and-end-all of New York, and it ran a hundred performances, with a little help from its producers, which was quite respectable. It wasn't enough to make it any sort of money, but it didn't do me too much harm, personally. And it certainly restored Phil Silvers, who went on to do bigger and better things.

But I wouldn't want to ever go round on tour again with a pre-New York run. The tensions are enormous. There's so much at stake, a fantastic amount at stake, in money and in reputations. You see American actors, particularly the less starry ones, who realise that a Broadway chance may come once, and it matters so much. The most painful part was the auditioning for the smaller parts, particularly for the girl playing Mary. We chose a girl called Jeanne Hepple eventually. We went through an enormous number of girls, and it was heartbreaking the amount it mattered to them: there were tears and all sorts of things. It's not very nice, auditioning, anyway, saying: 'Sorry, but no.' But in this case, because we wanted to be sure, we kept calling people back, then we got down to two. By that time, they were bringing their own props, their own costumes, changing in the loo and everything; and we both, Gene and I, sat there when we'd finished and chosen Jeanne and we were so depressed we got absolutely smashed at Frankie and Johnnie's. 'What an awful business we're in,' said Gene.

IW   How was Phil Silvers?

AA   Well, Phil was an amazing figure. This is the fate of the star system: Robert Morley having shaped the play as it was, we then looked for a man to play it on Broadway. And eventually, after going through an awful lot of people, somebody came up with the idea of Phil Silvers. He had disappeared for a bit: he hadn't been in the public eye. Sergeant Bilko he was still well loved for, and he'd got one or two Broadway successes like *Top Banana* under his belt, but that was some time ago; and nobody knew much about him. We found out about Phil that he was *(a)* an extremely nervous man and *(b)* an extremely nice man. But he'd had some form of nervous breakdown: he'd had – what can I call it? – a relapse, anyway. His marriage had broken up and it had upset him enormously; and he'd got a lot of daughters, all of whom he adored and never saw, because he wasn't allowed to. Anyway, he saw in this a chance – and I think everyone saw in it a chance for him – to reconstitute himself. But it was a bit therapeutic, like all these occasions.

First of all, what had gone was his memory: he couldn't remember any of the lines. *How The Other Half* was a tour I followed very, very closely: I was with the play more than I would ever be nowadays – I know better. I came over for the early rehearsals: and Gene Saks was a man who worked day and night really hard. Anyway, I left them in the early part of rehearsals, and it all looked pretty good. I came back at the beginning of the last week and I saw a run; and it didn't look any different from when I left it. So Gene and I went out and had a cup of coffee, and he said: 'What do you think?' And I said: 'Well, er, what's been going on for three weeks?' He sat there for a very long time and I thought I'd really upset him. He suddenly thumped the table and said: 'I don't know what's been going on for three weeks. What the blazes *has* been going on for three weeks?' he said. 'Nothing's been going on for three weeks! I'm going to go in there and tell them nothing's been going on for three weeks.' So he went back and said: 'Listen! This man has come back from England, and he's just said: 'Nothing's been going on for three weeks.' We're opening in a week, for God's sake.' And it turned out that one of the things that hadn't been happening for three weeks was that Phil hadn't learned his lines yet. They'd delegated an associate director to work with him – a man who crops up a lot in my life: he first cropped up as Peter Bridge's assistant, then turned up as Gene Saks' assistant, and is now Peggy Ramsay's assistant, Tom Erhardt. Tom is like a sort of lucky mascot, he turns up in various disguises. At this point he was in his native America, assisting Gene Saks. And assisting Gene Saks mainly meant sitting up with Phil Silvers every night and hearing his lines, until he was absolutely cross-eyed with them. Phil was in an extremely neurotic state. We found he was taking valium, which wasn't helping.

The first date on the tour was Palm Beach, the Playhouse there. And we'd got Phil as far as the third act, the last scene; so we had three scenes which we felt he could get through, with a little bit of help from his friends, but after that . . . So we said: 'Well, OK, we'll get

Sandy Dennis and Phil Silvers in the Broadway production of *How the Other Half Loves*

there. We can rely on the prompter for a week.' Palm Beach has the reputation of being the worst place anywhere. The whole audience is made up of socialites, all of whom leave after the interval: they never see the second half. The thing was that their chauffeurs were ordered back at the interval. They'd have their champagne reception when they were photographed extensively, and then they'd all leave. It was a terrible place. But it was my first taste of Florida, and it was very interesting to get there, suddenly zooming out of New York – in I suppose it was January – into sunshine.

We were a little flummoxed when we saw the stage, because it did not allow for a prompter. It was, like a lot of American stages, about 180 feet across. It was enormously wide, with an enormous forestage, and a big, billowing curtain like a maternity dress that came round the front. There was nowhere that you could have a prompter without a loudhailer, because the prompt corner was miles from the centre of the stage. So we looked at it, and this very old producer we had called Michael Myerberg – one of those men who would be played by Gabby Hayes, you know, and who'd seen everything before; a marvellous old boy, but one of those men who just couldn't be told – said: 'Well, we'll cut a hole in the forestage.' But the carpenter said: 'No, you can't cut a hole in the forestage: it's aluminium. It's an aluminium stage. You're cutting through pure aluminium there.' Myerberg said: 'I don't care about the cost. We're having a trap, like an opera box, in the front of the stage.' So they cut this hole, amidst great protest, and down into this hole went Tom Erhardt with the book, because we'd made no allowance for a prompter. And when he went down this hole, he was down there from the beginning to the end, because there was no way he could get out. Well, Tom is blond and fair and thinning, and when they put the lights on, you had this bright, shining head in the middle of the forestage; and it looked slightly prominent! Everyone said: 'What's that?' Myerberg said: 'We've got to darken down his head: it's reflecting the light.' So Tom was equipped with a black beret, which made him look not unlike a Provisional IRA man, crouching in a slit trench. And there he is with his script when we get to the first night. Phil's going great guns: he's doing very well. And the play is going so well that quite a lot of the chauffeurs are actually told to hold on at the interval. And the manager is ecstatic. But to show the sort of people they were, they'd actually failed to reserve a seat for the director or the author: we had nowhere to sit. Gene was furious. He said: 'How are we going to get this play right when we're not allowed to see it?' So there's a great kerfuffle. He said: 'I demand that the author and I see the first night. We want to see it. We want to know how to do the second night!' So they find us a place, and it's way, way up behind the front-of-house lights, which are in a sort of loft. Behind wire mesh we sat crouching by these big beasts that were burning up – 5,000 kilowatt lamps! – sweating and peering through the mesh, clinging on, feeling slightly giddy; and we were back, a long way back. And the big maternity dress draws round again in the scene change before the last scene; and it's a thin dress, it's not a thick curtain. And you can hear through the curtain Phil's voice shouting down to Tom in his hole: 'I need you now, baby!' Which, of course, comes ringing into the auditorium.

We'd had one marvellous incident just before that, when Bernice Massi, who played Fiona, had brought on the frigadella and served it, and parked her trolley without allowing for the rake. It had rolled away from her, very slowly tipped off the end of the forestage and covered two of the most beautiful American people – a blonde in a strapless evening dress and her escort in full dinner jacket. Covered them in frigadella. That was tremendous, and that stopped the show for some minutes while they mopped themselves down and put this whole trolley back on the stage. The audience loved that, they thought it was terrific. They thought it was meant.

So, the curtains drew and Phil starts the last scene, and certainly cues are coming thick and fast and people are covering; and then he gets to one line, which was one of those lines that nobody could help him on. He says: 'Well, I . . . I . . . I . . . think, Bob, that . . . I think, Bob, that . . . that . . . ' And Tom, the prompter, is not a prompter. There's a great art in prompting, to give the right key word and to give it quickly and cleanly. And Tom has a very loud voice, and a very slow voice. So Tom gives him: 'Possibly.' Phil, by then, you can see, has got buzzing noises in his ears, and he couldn't hear if you actually screamed it at him. He said: 'I think . . . I think, Bob . . . I . . . I . . . ' And Tom's voice comes again, equally loudly: 'Possibly!' 'Just that . . . I think . . . I think, Bob . . . er . . . you know, Bob . . . ' And a man, right at the back of the theatre, shouts: 'Possibly!' Gene says: 'Oh my god, the audience are prompting him now!' At the end of the show, we walked round and round the block. Phil was prostrate: 'The humiliation! I'm a man who made millions laugh on Bilko.' 'It's all right, Phil, don't worry, we all have bad nights.' 'Bad night! I've been prompted by the audience!'

Later on, I got very fond of Phil. Just before we went into New York, Sandy Dennis said: 'We must do something about Phil. He looks so terrible. He dresses so badly. Can't we get him into some decent clothes?' Phil's heard this eventually and he's very hurt. So we're driving into New York. He said: 'You realise you're working with a man who's unbalanced. I mean, I am unbalanced, I admit it.' I said: 'No, you're not unbalanced, Phil. You're nervous, because you're going into New York and you don't know what's going to happen to you.' He said. 'I tell you I'm unbalanced.' I said: 'No, you're not.' He said: 'What man who wasn't unbalanced would wear this tie with these socks?'

He opened, and the play got reasonable reviews. He was very good eventually, but it was such hard work to get Phil to that pitch. What one was pleased about was that we reconstituted a very funny artist. I saw him some three years later, still the fall-guy. He was playing in Bournemouth – *A Funny Thing Happened On the Way To The Forum*. And I happened to be there, visiting my kids at school. I said: 'It can't be Phil Silvers.' And I went along, and there was old Phil, with an audience, I suppose, a quarter full, giving absolutely everything. It was a super evening. And so I whistled round to see him. Kenneth Tynan was also round there: he knew Phil and admired him. I said: 'Terrific to see you. I'd no idea you were in Bournemouth.' He said: 'Well, there's been a foul-up, baby. You see, I'd understood I was coming over here to tour prior to a West End appearance.' I said: 'Oh, you're going to bring this into town?' He said: 'Well, I understood this.' I said: 'But it's been in, with Bob Monkhouse.' He said: 'I know. I didn't find that out till I got to Norwich.' Poor old Phil.

IW   He's still around, isn't he?

AA   Yes. And he's still very funny. He just needs to be better informed.

THE BUSINESS OF WRITING

IW   You schedule a new play up to a year ahead, don't you? How much do you know at that stage about what the play's going to be?

AA   I have an idea. As soon as I've finished a play – once I finished, say, *Suburban Strains*, I was raring to go on another, keyed up and ready. You get on a tremendous high – I do – from writing, when you think: 'Wow! I can write for ever!' Actually, somebody at the back of you says: 'Oh no, you can't!' But nevertheless, that's the time I schedule the next one and say: 'I must get another one done.' And at that point there's a few sketched ideas. It may be off-the-shelf ideas.

IW   What do you mean by that? Things you've filed away over the years?

AA   Filed away. The *Taking Steps* idea was an idea that had been on that bloody shelf for years. The thing that was missing was the three floors. Once I'd got the three floors, then the other idea went *Dooiing*! – about a man whose wife left him and another guy read the farewell letter. It sounds like the crudest idea in the world, but that was the nub of the whole play.

IW   So at what stage do you decide that you're going to take something off the shelf, or look for something totally new?

AA   Not until I get there.

IW   In the intervening period, which one might think of as a gestation period and which can indeed be exactly nine months, nothing happens, does it? You don't start making notes or drawing complicated plans?

AA   No. I usually treasure a sort of surrogate child, who gets thrown out of the nest as the time gets closer. I say: 'This is a wonderful idea.' I get closer to it, and the wonderful idea suddenly, as I sit down with a new sheet of paper, appears to be nothing but useless. And then I scramble round for the other idea that may have been lurking behind it. I've sat down with certain ideas time and again and never written them: I've written the idea that's been behind them. Things keep happening. Things add to an idea. It feels like a stone and it rolls; and little things stick on it. I need about eight ideas – well, not quite eight, but I need several – to make a play. I'm not happy when there's just one sitting there. For instance, take the example I gave you about *Taking Steps*: I'm not happy when I just have an idea about a wife leaving a man and him inviting another bloke in to read the letter. I need two more, like the bedrooms, and the man who drives everyone to sleep; and when I've got those three going together, then I think: 'Now we'll be able to get something to happen. Now the chemistry's flowing for a play, as opposed to a sketch.' And often the ideas I've got are sketch ideas: they don't attract other ideas like chemistry. So I dump them or shelve them until such time as they attract little friends, who together make a whole! That seems to be what happens. And it's often just a matter of assembling the right sequence of things together.

IW   Have you got any formula for getting these ideas in the first place? Presumably they accrete quite in spite of yourself a lot of the time. But where do they come from in the first place?

AA   God knows. They come in the most extraordinary ways. But I forget a lot of them actually.

IW   You don't write them down?

AA   No. I'm just annoyed at the moment, as I'm talking to you: something wonderful struck me the other day, and I can't remember what the hell it was. Ah, never mind: it'll come back.

IW   You don't often lose them forever?

AA   It's somewhere locked in here. Somewhere. The trouble is, because I don't tell anyone else, I can't actually check it! I always suspect that a new one will pop up if it's right.

IW   Most of your plays, quite apart from their ostensible subject matter, have got a very strong craft element in them. On one level at least, they're about the whole nature of theatrical artifice. The sort of things I'm thinking of are the combination stagescape, as in *How The Other Half Loves* and *Taking Steps*; equally the dumb show in Act Two of *Absurd Person Singular*, which is actually credible only as a stage device. Is it possible to separate that craft element from the evolution of the plays themselves? In other words, when the play's germinating, do you tend to work from thematic ideas or from some technical challenge that you've got to overcome?

Sheila Hancock and Anna Calder-Marshall in *Absurd Person Singular* in the West End

AA Well, they seem to go together; I think *how* to tell the story to me is always very important. And I always look for new ways. I am peculiarly attracted to the stage. Probably more than most writers, I write exclusively for one medium. I love the permutations that it possesses and I love exploring them. And particularly I'm fascinated by things like how it presents time, and how its space can be changed, and the peculiarity which it possesses that, when you warp time on stage, you're warping time for an audience as well as for the actors – you're doing it positively, in front of people's eyes. It's not like television when one's used to jumping three years; on stage, the way you do it is much more immediate. All these elements are very important. And I think, in the best plays, the idea and the technique come together: one wants to write something, the idea is glimmering, then the how presents itself – how do I tell this story? In *Sisterly Feelings*, I wanted to write about choice, and then came the thought that this was the time to use that particular device, precisely because it was about choice.

IW The device of tossing the coin?

AA Tossing the coin and choosing, and thus varying the play. I'm also, I suppose, reacting to my own peculiar theatre, where I couldn't have written *Rookery Nook* even if I'd wanted to, because I haven't got any doors. And so I've got to find some farcical equivalent. The thing with plays is selection: you've got to find how to tell your story best. It may be you do it with one set, continuous action (as in *Absent Friends*), and real time (moving from point A to, an hour and a half later, point B – that's the simplest). Then there are things like *Suburban Strains*, where I wanted to tell a very complex story – well, it's actually very simple, but I wanted to highlight it in a different way. I've always had this ambition to run parallel times; and here was the chance to do that, by starting a story simultaneously in the middle and at the beginning and running parallel.

IW The technique is basically filmic there, isn't it?

AA Yes, a lot of my stuff is obviously filched from film. The thing about film is that it's developed its own tense-flexibility: what I do is pre-edit, as it were, with plays. I'm fascinated by techniques and by being aware that what I want to say is relatively simple; that is, it's usually telling about people and about their relationships. In order to throw any light – or at least fresh slants – it's necessary to find new ways to tell the stories.

IW I wonder if there's a risk involved. Thinking again of *Absurd Person Singular*, which is a play about social reversal – social and professional reversal – is there any danger that the use of tricks, which is basically what the second act was, can in some way devalue what it is you're saying through the theme of the play? In other words, is there a danger that the craft

To mark the success of *Absurd Person Singular* on Broadway, the City of New York renamed one of its streets.

can negate the theme of the play, simply by being too bloody clever?

AA   Oh yes, I think so. One's in this Scylla and Charybdis situation, because if I tell my stories terribly solemnly and seriously, or without any of this stuff, nobody wants to see them. I've really got to make them entertaining. I've really got to make them eye-catching, not in a garish sense, but in an absorbing sense so that people say: 'Golly, I was held from beginning to end.' And it's up to me to employ whatever technical resources I have; but I always try to be extremely careful that the technical resources do not deny the characters their true destinies. I hope that they always proceed with a certain dignity, so that their destinies are fulfilled without unnecessary author's interruptions and awful detours in order to get cheap laughs. I hope that rarely do characters say things that they would not normally say, in order to make a laugh. A lot of my writing is involved in actually avoiding such tempting moments, when you could, for the sake of five more lines, get a very big laugh, but would then leave the character without one leg to stand on later in the scene – I'm desperately trying to avoid these moments. If I do use a device, I hope it enhances rather than detracts, that's all I can say.

IW – The classic example of that was the device which came half-way through the writing of *Absurd Person Singular*. What happened there? You started by setting it in the sitting room?

AA   Yes; and swopped it to the kitchen. That comes back to selection. The whole of playwriting for me is, if you like: you get your idea, you get your sequence of events –which, if written literally, would take, say, four days at least to perform on stage – and you then have to select what you want your audience to see, preferably the minimum to allow them to understand the events. It seems to me that economy in writing is more and more desirable: if you could tell a story or draw a picture with four lines, then so be it, let's do it, let's make it the ultimate short story. Unfortunately, no-one's quite clever enough – certainly I'm not clever enough – to do that yet.

IW   I suppose one of the great paradoxes about you – since I guess you're probably the most prolific living playwright in English – is that you spend very little time indeed actually writing, don't you? You spend – what? – at most about two weeks over the writing of a play?

AA   I lay aside four and write for two.

IW   And you don't work from notes made over a longer period. Can we just take it step by step? What occurs during your period of creative retreat? First of all, you pay all the bills, you shut the doors, close the windows and you don't see anyone. Is that right?

AA   Yes. I say: 'Look, loves. I'm out of commission for a month.' I suppose for about the first week or ten days I don't do anything very much: I wander around and read and sharpen pencils, watch telly; I do all the normal things – fix shelves, things like that. I go for walks, moon around . . .

IW   Is this a thought process?

AA   Yes, a thought process; a sort of sifting process, really.

IW   It's not just avoiding the issue?

AA   It is avoiding the issue, partly, yes. But it's also knowing it's going to come, but there's no hurry. That's the sort of feeling.

Absurd Person Singular in Scarborough

IW   Well how do you know it's going to come, and why is there no hurry? Because manifestly there is, when at this stage you're already scheduled to get into rehearsal on a specific date at a specific hour in four weeks' time. Why are you not suffering the most appalling pressures and taking all sorts of tranquillizing medicaments?

AA   Well, one's worrying, in a sort of way. But I know that there's no way I'd start a play four weeks before it's due to go on. That just isn't the way I write. I know I've got to be within single figures of the opening date before there's any chance. So, really, with twenty-eight days, I've got eighteen days at least to go before I start to write.

IW   Why?

AA   I don't know. I've got to finish it just before it starts.

IW   You can't start it earlier and take longer over the process?

AA   No. If I get time for re-thinking – I'm a really ferocious critic of my own work, I really am – I would destroy it. There's no way it would survive if it didn't have to survive just in order for there to be something there.

IW   Right, so you're pottering around, watching television and putting shelves up and so on; and getting irritable?

AA   A bit. Not too bad, to start with. I usually have a notepad at hand on which I draw primitive designs. Probably the shape I'm working on is the shape of the aforesaid original idea, that I was thinking about eight months ago and trying to work. Nine times out of ten, that idea will be jettisoned like some old skin, and I just hope to god there's something underneath. Occasionally, I then have a frenzied ferret through the shelves of my mind for other previously rejected ideas which suddenly spring forward – as, after desperate raking, I came across the old *Taking Steps* idea which had been thrown out before. An idea keeps popping up like a weed in the garden; you lop its head off and next year back it is again! There are other times when I'm actually much more committed to an idea, as with *Bedroom Farce*. I was committed to writing a play about bedrooms, though I didn't actually know what to write about bedrooms until I started.

IW   How, committed?

AA   Well, I'd said I wanted to write about bedrooms and I'd announced the title.

94

IW The title's something I wanted to ask you about, because the first thing anyone ever hears of any of your plays is the title, which seems to come at a very early stage of your retreat.

AA Yes.

IW And some of your titles are very weird anyway. Though they're very memorable as titles, they don't necessarily have anything very much to do with what's in the play. You once told me that *Absurd Person Singular* was actually the title of a totally different play; you kept the title and changed the play.

AA Yes, I liked the title.

IW It's a smashing title, but it hasn't actually got anything to do with the play. Do you think of the titles as a totally separate game?

AA Sometimes. Some of them are quite easy to come by, and some of them are more difficult. Sometimes the titles arrive half-way through the play, sometimes they arrive before the play's even thought of. It depends. *Joking Apart* was before the play was thought of; *Bedroom Farce* way before the play was written; *Suburban Strains* half-way through; *Taking Steps* – oh yes – after it had started, so, in fact, quite apt.

IW Do you have a deadline when you say: 'Right, I'm actually going to sit down, and that paper in front of me is going to start being filled'?

AA I have two or three nights when I realise I'm getting very close. It's always nights. I don't start until the sun's gone down, probably ten o'clock at night.

IW And you write through the night?

AA I try to. I tend to get later and later. Probably, the first night, I sit down at ten and go to bed at two, very disgruntled because I've written nothing. The next night, after a frustrating day moping around, I sit down at ten and I might work till three, and still have written nothing. And then one night, I might write half an act, a third of a play; it depends how it goes. Normally, I probably start quite slowly – write a quarter of a play; if the play isn't working, I tend to start the second draft before I've finished the first, in an attempt to shake it.

IW That is all in longhand, is it?

Alan Ayckbourn
Wesołych Świąt
!!! xx*
ŚWIĘTA!
teatr dramatyczny m.st. warszawy

AA The first draft is in longhand; but for instance, with *Ten Times Table*, I was getting very stuck. I was into page 90 on my foolscap, thinking: 'I can't get this clear.' So I said to Heather, my assistant: 'I think I'll want to dictate tonight.' Heather always keeps herself clear. And so we sat down and I started to dictate from the notes, through all the dialogue. And that's the second draft.

IW How different is it from the first draft?

AA Oh, vastly. Unrecognisable. You can pick up a page and, if you could read it, you might recognise where it came from in the play – you might not.

IW You dictate it to Heather, and Heather types it straight off.

AA Yes, quite slowly. What might happen is that she types during the night, she goes to bed, and by that time – I've found of late – I can actually work during the daytime. I sit down and write, perhaps, some more during the day.

IW Of the first draft?

AA Yes, and then dictate it to her as a second draft. That's quite a nice way of working: it's less lonely. I'm always finding ways not to be quite so alone writing. As soon as I can get on to the second draft, I'm actually kidding myself that I've finished it. Although, of course, I haven't. In fact, I've been known quite often to throw out a whole act of a second draft and the thing remains very fluid until the moment when it's bound and delivered. Anyway the excitement from doing the second draft stimulates me into doing more of the first draft. And actually talking the characters, there come points when you *can* talk about the play. I remember having dictated the second draft of the first act of *Absurd Person Singular* and Heather asking: 'Where are we going next?' I said: 'We're going into the Jacksons' kitchen, and I thought I'd have this dog outside the door.' By that stage, one is sharing the idea. Then I went off and wrote that. That was a strange play: I wrote that while I was rehearsing during the day. I was much younger then.

IW Rehearsing what?

AA I was rehearsing the first play of the Scarborough season, called *Carmilla*, by David Campton. *Absurd Person* was the second play to go in. I remember going into a rehearsal of *Carmilla* and saying: 'Anybody know any forfeits?' And somebody said: 'Orange between the knees.' And I said: 'Oh, thanks very much!' People in the cast wondered what was going on! That's how that was done. So that's the second draft: dictation.

Poster for the Warsaw production of *Absurd Person Singular*

IW   And you get right the way through and finish the play in second draft form?

AA   Yes. It's then a pile of typescript. Then I have to brace myself because we're getting very near, probably, to rehearsal by now.

IW   In fact, you might be there by now.

AA   Yes, I might be, indeed, into the first day. I then sit down and read it through. Probably there's quite a lot to do on it – not vast re-writes in the sense that we pull out fifty pages, but every page has probably got something to be altered on it. I generally find this with dictating. Occasionally it's very good for effect, but obviously you don't want to use the same word eight times in a sentence, just because you're not aware what you've said, or because you've lost the thread.

IW   Do you do the voices and the accents as you dictate?

AA   Yes, I tend to: I certainly soften off on the women. Heather says occasionally: 'I can always hear the way you dictated that: they never played it quite the same.' Fortunately, I personally lose those rhythms very quickly, otherwise it would be unbearable to work with an actor on them.
   That's the crucial draft, the dictated one, and that just takes off.

IW   And the third draft is . . .

AA   Correction. Musing upon it, shaping it, clearing up the odd bit, clarifying it. Correcting silly things, like calling a bloke Gordon in the first act and Geoffrey in the second – little things like that. And then, just the duplication.

IW   And how sacrosanct is the script thereafter? Is it freeze-dried or is the company allowed – do you allow yourself – to make revisions within rehearsal?

AA   It very rarely changes, I must say. I suppose, to be fair, the actors are rather wary now. At one stage, when I was very new, the actors wanted to change everything: they all wanted to put their three-ha'porth in. Now they learn my spelling mistakes! So I have to say: 'No, no, I didn't actually mean that, love. That's the name of the play next week – it got printed at the bottom by mistake!' Of course there are occasions when I change things. But I have the same attitude to my plays as I suppose someone who's just finished a picture must have – that the composition is as it is because it is as it is. While I was writing it, I very carefully put my figures in this particular landscape in this particular order. And one must

Just Between Ourselves at the Gladsaxe Teater, Søborg, Denmark

Just Between Ourselves at the Nieuwe de la Mar Theater te Amsterdam, Holland

assume certain things: my technique by now must be fairly good, and therefore the figures are recognisable, and if they're there where they are, it's because that's how I painted them. In a sense, if I have to do something radical like move a figure, I'd sooner re-write the play. So no, nothing gets changed very much in rehearsal. Things get clarified, things get explored. There are occasionally additions, as when I took *Absent Friends* away and wrote two or three pages; in the case of *Just Between Ourselves* I inserted a whole scene.

IW   In rehearsal?

AA   After it had been read. There's a scene in act two with Pam and Dennis, in which she says: 'Do you think I'm attractive, Dennis?' And he replies: 'Ah, well, I'd certainly fancy you, but I'm a married man.' That scene wasn't there initially. I don't quite know how it worked without it, but at the time that's how it was. I think what happens sometimes is that something's in my head but it's not on the page! That was a very odd case of a whole scene I certainly thought I'd written: I looked and it wasn't there. The actors read it quite happily; but I think they might have questioned it when they started to work on it.

   In *Absent Friends* I re-wrote something that didn't work: I wrote something rather sentimental by mistake and snatched it back, then wrote the proper scene: the scene between Paul and Colin towards the end. If I make my character voluble and eloquent, I'm always doomed. I gave Paul a sort of manic laugh, which did the whole thing for me and said what I wanted to say. That's where one learns about playwriting, to say: 'Oh, come on, the audience already knows that, you've told them that.' The nice thing is to spread clues and spread them quite thinly, and allow the audience to gather them. I think an audience responds to that. It's a joy to put something down, then see it picked up. And maybe you don't know it's being picked up until twenty minutes later, when some reference is made and the audience reacts. You say: 'They did get that. That's marvellous!' And you're never quite sure: you hope they do, and you set it up so that it should work.

There's a very interesting example in *Bedroom Farce*, I remember, which you could perhaps say is a crude one. Trevor goes into the bedroom at the end, and Kate says:'Look what Malcolm made for me.' And it's that chest of drawers. We did it on the first night – and we'd pissed ourselves laughing in rehearsal about this collapsing chest of drawers– and Chris Godwin crossed to it and picked it up, and it all fell to bits. And there's a very desultory laugh. And we said: 'What happened? What happened to our expensive prop and no laugh?' Then it occurred to me that you must give the audience just enough time to anticipate what he was going to do. What was going on in their minds could never be capped by what was going to happen to four pieces of timber. So on the second night, I just said: 'Be nearer that piece of furniture and put your hands on it *before* . . . and then they're with you.' And he did that and it was a belter.

IW   Yes, the alternative to that, of course, is the second act of *Absurd Person Singular*, where everybody in the audience knows, a full twenty minutes before it happens, that someone's going to get drenched underneath that sink, because you set that one up. Yet when it eventually happens, it's at a beautiful moment.

AA   Yes, that's always fun. Try and mislead them twice, and then make out you're not going to play the gag, then do it. *Taking Steps* is full of running gags – there are thousands of them, all running at once. Somebody called them repetitive, which I thought was a bit rude. But audiences love running gags.

IW   When you talk about your writing, you sound as if you're not terribly fond of it and writing is actually just another way of directing.

AA   Well, I don't like a lot of writing. When things are working, it's extraordinary. And quite often I find when I'm writing a play, for the first half I'm spewing out things which I then reap later. Mark, in *Taking Steps*, for example, has a characteristic where, whenever he talks earnestly and seriously about his relationship, everybody else falls asleep: his voice

gets duller and duller. It's sort of tragic and slightly removed from the truth, but nonetheless everyone knows people like that – you are aware they are talking seriously but your mind wanders. So here he is, this tragic man, who is doomed like some Ancient Mariner to see people nodding off as he speaks, and I thought: 'This is fun'. So I put him into the first scene. I had no idea how I was going to use it again, but was joyous when I got later on, into a scene where Roland has taken sleeping pills and they have to keep him awake; and I said: 'Oh! I've got a man who sends people to sleep in this scene! This is wonderful!' I was so pleased that the two elements had been on a collision course; but I had no idea when I started the play that would happen. That was terribly enjoyable.

But on the whole it's a lone and boring business. I don't know how novelists manage, because they never get to share their business with anybody. I actually get in there – admittedly, I also stand to be knocked down – with a group of actors. You share your writing with them and discuss it and work it and, hopefully, if things are going well, they get fond of it too and find the things funny that you found funny. Then, eventually, an audience – and that's marvellous.

IW   Did radio never appeal to you as a medium?

AA   No. Frankly, I didn't know what the job was when I applied to join the BBC. I thought I was going to be sorting out Alfred Bradley's filing. But it seemed quite a good way to pass a little bit of time while I thought about what to do after *Whatnot*. When I got there I found that, far from sorting out Alfred's filing, I was going to be doing my own programmes and running with a great deal more responsibility than I'd had in the theatre. I think the single most important thing it gave me was the moment when, with a little bit of guidance from knowledgeable secretaries and other people, I was actually going to put a whole show together. I was to book the artists, book the studio, and do all that sort of business: it was almost like a finishing school.

Radio itself, I must say, I went into without enormous enthusiasm, although I'd been a great listener as a child. But once in, I found it was a magic place. At that particular point in the history of the BBC, it was such a backwater (television was the place) that you could work totally unobserved doing the most interesting things. It did two things: it gave me a great opportunity to do far more plays – I did more plays in a year than I'd done in ten years in the theatre – and it also foisted upon me the occasional plays that I didn't want to do, which, of course, in the theatre you can generally avoid because you don't accept them. And it's quite good occasionally to do a play you don't want to do. You actually have to learn a little bit of technique: you've got to keep the actors going, just for the length of the play. They know it's bad, you know it's bad, but if you ever admit it, it's gone. And some of my best work was done on those things.

IW It wasn't at that stage as technical a medium as it is now, insofar as it wasn't stereo, was it? It was purely monaural. Did you feel that you explored the medium as a medium?

AA Oh yes, very much, because I was fascinated by sound. I had, of course, with *Whatnot*, been a tape recorder freak. There was some wonderful equipment there and we had great fun with the gear.

IW Were you at all influenced by Alfred?

AA Not production-wise, though I was influenced by him in other ways. Alfred's strongest point was obviously his relationship with his writers. And I suppose I learnt from him a certain amount about how to treat writers, and how to draw them out, though I don't think I've got the perseverance or the dedication to do what he does. There were the maxims he had: if you want a play, you've got to go and get it. The unsolicited scripts are never any good: nobody ever sends you *Under Milk Wood*. You've got to go out and sit in Dylan Thomas's pub until he writes it. And all his plays came that way, of course, as a result of his doggedly driving around in his large Rover and parking on people's doorsteps. I'd already been working with actors of course, and I suppose I had learnt the hard way about directing them. But now I learnt something about writers.

IW But you never felt moved to write for radio yourself?

AA No. I think I was dealing so actively all day with writers that I felt first it would almost be cheating to write my own plays for radio. And I also wasn't actually very inspired to do so. I did try one script, which I sent to Colin Shaw (the Head of North Region, now at the IBA) when I'd just joined; but he wasn't very keen, and I wasn't very keen on it either, so I gave it up.

IW Since leaving, the medium hasn't attracted you at all?

AA No. It's a narrative medium, it's a different sort of medium, it's not mine. I'm really too basically a visual writer for that.

IW You did once write – and this was ten years later – a television play. And only one.

AA Oh, that was ridiculous. I happen to have a very close friend who comes to all our first nights, called Herbert Wise. He's a well-known television director, who'd been landed with a series for BBC2, called *Masquerade*. Some boffin in the back room had this great idea. He said: 'Let's ask about half a dozen jolly writers to write a play around a fixed theme – like a fancy dress party.' So Herbie said: 'Look, it's half an hour: here's the theme. Please, I'd love to do your first telly.' And I said: 'Well, it's very nice of you, Herbie.' And half an hour, actually, is twenty-eight pages: it's really a night's work. So I said: 'Well, look, I must see the producers. I must talk about this, because I don't know anything about it.' So they dutifully showed me round the studios. And I said: 'Well, could you just give me some idea of the cast requirements and the set?' And they said: 'We've got this wonderful new lightweight video camera, so really, don't worry about the sets. You write what you want to do in half an hour: we will film it.' I said: 'Oh, that's wonderful. What about cast?' They said: 'You write what you want: we will cast it. We don't want you to be hampered by physical conditions. Just write.' So I went away and I wrote this play for twenty-four people. It roved all over this bloody hotel: there were about thirty-eight sets. So, silence. 'Ah,' they said, 'well, we didn't think you'd write twenty-four people.' So I cut it down to eighteen and simplified the sets. But, of course, the budget of the series was already costed and so the whole thing was pitifully under-financed. And, because of the technical complexities which I'd set, Herbie, on location – two days in a pub in Berkshire – was having his work cut out: some scenes he never got in the can at all, because he had no time! So, it was OK, but it was very far from what it was intended originally to be – a waiter's eye-view of a dreadful office party.

IW   You gave up after that, did you?

AA   I didn't find it very enjoyable. At the point when the thing was being done and I was used to being most involved, I was sitting in a van with a bloke who was recording it. He was watching the budget on ITV, and watching my play out of the corner of his eye, just to see when they said: 'Roll VTR'. Then he went back to the budget again. He said: 'What is all this?' I said: 'Well, it's a play, actually.' 'Oh yes? What's it about then?' I said: 'Well, I wrote it.' He said: 'Oh, did you? Is it any good?' I said: 'Well, yes, it's about this . . . ' and I actually talked to him for about half an hour about it. By the end, he was shouting ideas down the line, and they were saying: 'Thank you very much, VTR: we can manage, thank you.' It wasn't a very good way to spend your play.

I only want to be up there directing – and I really can't be bothered to start taking television directors' courses at this time of life – or I don't want to know. The interesting bit's directing, not writing.

IW   And to date, anyway, no film screenplays.

AA   The British film industry's nearly dead: that's the only one I could ever have written for. I suppose if Ealing Studios had been going at full flourish, and if they'd been interested enough to approach me and say: 'Would you like to be another Tibby Clark and write a few *Lavender Hill Mobs*?' with the studio of talents they had at that time, it would have been

PLAYS AND THEMES

IW You started writing very soon after the angry revolution – John Osborne, John Arden, Ann Jellicoe. That crew suddenly hit the Royal Court in 1956 and were making really rather a lot of noise in the British theatre. You seem to have been affected not at all by them in what you were writing at that time. Were you aware of them and what they were doing?

AA Yes, I think I was, but not immediately, perhaps. Although they were writing then, I was starting in rep where they hadn't yet arrived. We were still tending to do Agatha and *The Grand National Night*, and all those sort of thrillers: we'd alternate thriller-comedy-thriller-comedy. So I suppose that my instant exposure was to the more conventional drama of the time. It wasn't until I ran personally into people like H. Pinter that things really began to take a grip. He certainly did affect me. I was also influenced by boyhood fads of the time. At this point, I remember – it doesn't show either – I was influenced a lot by Pirandello and Ionesco and Anouilh. I was very keen on Anouilh. I liked the way he constructed. I was very drawn to the craftsmen of the business. Although I liked the content, I was perhaps slightly less impressed by the techniques displayed by some of the new wave, because it did seem that a lot of things were thrown out simply because they smacked of Rattigan, who, poor man, went to his grave with 'well-made-play' being shouted at him. But occasionally, when you sat through one, you thought: 'Thank god for the well-made play,' because the evening did at least come to a successful resolution, even if one quibbled with some of the content.

Priestley I liked. But it was only later that I began to see the other side. Pinter was enormously influential, simply because his history is that of an actor and of a poet, then a writer, a playwright. And I sense that the actor-poet is still what he is; his use of language and his careful selection of words (which is something I was very impressed by and have tried to copy), is so fascinating and yet so eloquent, so delicate, that it had an immediate effect on me. My selection of words is far more, I suppose, sly than his: he will use a word more stylistically. I'll bury words. But on occasions you'll find, I think, similarities.

IW In the earlier plays, the critics in Yorkshire, anyway, were tending to talk about you in terms of Noel Coward.

AA Well, there's a similarity, but it came after *Relatively Speaking*. And at that point I really was still formulating a style. I always say to writers, although sometimes they don't believe me, I don't honestly think there's any harm in being influenced by, and indeed in copying to a certain extent, people you admire. I didn't actually copy Noel Coward; I mean, I didn't intend to. Looking back on it, I can quite see why *Relatively Speaking* was compared to Noel Coward. But what I was trying to do was something that Stephen Joseph had told me to do: 'For once in your life, try and write a well-made play.'

However, I suppose a lot that influenced me has nothing to do with the theatre at all. *Whatnot* is the outstanding example, which was totally to do with films – people like René Clair and Renoir, and going back to Buster Keaton and Laurel and Hardy, who still remain, I suppose, my major comic influence. If I could write a latterday Laurel and Hardy film, I'd be absolutely delighted; or a latterday Laurel and Hardy play. A lot of my stuff is actually closer to that and to Keaton than I suspect it is to my contemporary comic dramatists.

IW You talk about your work as belonging to the popular theatre. That term needs a certain amount of definition, doesn't it, because the Popular Theatre, I guess, is what the left wing writers would say they were writing for – a working class theatre: a working class and intellectual audience, perhaps, which is not in any sense what you're meaning by popular theatre, is it?

AA No, but I don't actually think that established theatres have anything to do with the working class anyway. Of course, there's a sizeable minority of people from the working class who go to the theatre, but I don't in general think the working class want to know much about it. It smacks to them of culture and exclusiveness.

It's not so much a matter of class as of sex at the moment: the theatre is predominantly a middle class woman's occupation. The men in Scarborough that I meet say: 'I don't go, but the wife does' – it's the famous phrase. You say: 'Why don't you go?' 'Well, it's a bit highbrow for me,' they say. And you say: 'Oh, so you think your wife is more highbrow than you; I mean, that your wife is more intelligent than you?' 'No, of course she isn't.' I say: 'Well, what makes it so that she can understand it . . . ?' 'Well, she's into art, you know.' Art is such a dirty word in England, it really is. It's like it's poofy, it's female, it's elite, it's exclusive – I suppose that view has been encouraged because we're a nation of snobs, and we tend to make art exclusive. It's quite extraordinary to go to New York, for instance, in a fairly egalitarian artistic society, and see policemen going in to buy a seat in the theatre, in uniform – I thought we were being raided! – and not feeling stupid about it. And cab drivers saying: 'Oh, I saw that.' Ask an English cab driver to take you to the Lyric and he'll say: 'Where? Oh, it's a theatre, is it?'

I'm on a crusade to try and persuade people that theatre can be fun; but every time I start doing that, some hairy bugger from the left comes in and tells them it's instructive, and drives them all out again. If I want to be instructed, I go to night school. I may be instructed in the theatre, but I don't go in there predominantly for instruction: I go in there for entertainment, and of course all the best plays instruct me, or enlighten me – it's a better word than instruct. But if you put a label on a whisky bottle with 'For medicinal use only' on it, it rather puts you off the drink.

IW   The canvas you take in your plays tends therefore to reflect the people that you reckon are going to be coming into the theatre?

AA   No, that sounds as if I deliberately try and reflect the audience. I'm very lucky that my particular level of writing, class-wise, is slap-bang in the middle of the English theatre-going public. If I was a working class dramatist, I'd have a much harder time of it because my reflected audience would be that much smaller; I could overcome it, but it's a tougher battle. Then I'd be better off writing for television; people will watch unbelievable things on television – unbelievably deep, absorbing plays that they would never dream of going to the theatre to see. It's nothing to do with the play itself, I suspect, it's to do with the social act of going to the theatre.

Theatres go through awful convolutions trying to attract the working class. They make the theatre very dirty and very unpleasant and smelly, and they say. 'Well, this will encourage people: they won't think it's stuck-up rubbish.' But then, that's not the answer, because most people in the working class, particularly if they go out for the evening, want to put on their very best clothes and want to go somewhere very nice – hence their working men's clubs, which are some of the most magnificent buildings in the north, and the best appointed. So that's a myth. So, you then try and make it very comfortable and very pleasant, but then it begins to look a bit snooty, so I don't know quite how on earth you win the audience. The first thing you've got to do is to have very good draught beer. But where is the art in all this? Then the chaps will stay in the bar anyway! Stephen Joseph circled it for a long time, with his fish and chip theatre. But what you're then doing is actually not providing theatre: you're providing a *sort* of theatre. To me, theatre *is* an art; it has to be something that takes ninety per cent of your concentration, not eight per cent, otherwise you're providing music hall, variety or something else. They of course are very valid, very important forms of theatre, but it's not the same thing. All the plays I admire require at least silence.

IW   So you're in there, up to your elbows in the English middle class – or rather the English middle classes, because one of the things you do like is to find the internal hierarchies. I wonder where, in fact, you get them from nowadays? You spend so much time – in fact, you seem to spend all your time – in the theatre, rather than out in the suburban dining rooms which your plays examine.

Absent Friends at the Riksteatern, Solna, Sweden

AA   I get about a bit, because I live in a small enough town to do it. In London I probably wouldn't. In London, one tends to go from box A to box B. In Scarborough one tends to go to intermediate boxes and, because I am willy nilly drawn into some of the social life, because a lot of the people there know me by sight, a lot of chat goes on, a lot of socialising with audiences, a lot of opening of fetes. So I do hear English spoken, which is really the name of the game. And, of course actors are, after all, human beings too: one sometimes tends to forget that. It would be wrong to say they have *more* complicated lives, but they have lives every bit as complicated as people who aren't actors. Running a theatre means that you are forced to share a building with twenty-five other people, eight of whom are actors, and the rest of whom are in various classes of trade – wardrobe maintenance through to electrics. The company is very aware that a lot of what they do is picked up and used: there are a lot of smiles when we first read one of my new plays. The Vera syndrome, the knocking everything over: there were at least two actors who looked rather – well, they didn't look upset, but they smiled thinly.

The thing that I don't often stress is of course that – I don't know quite what the

110

percentage is, but I suspect it's very large – most of it is me. Now, I happen to have just about every single phobia and fault that anybody's ever had: I have them all. And I also am possessed, fortunately, with a sort of enormous detachment from myself, so that I can actually see myself doing it. As Tom says in *The Norman Conquests*: 'I let her down. I can feel myself doing it while I'm doing it.' I do a lot of that. And a lot of it's me.

IW   Would you accept that in *Relatively Speaking*, and perhaps other plays around that time, the natural habitat of the people was actually Shaftesbury Avenue rather than the world? In other words, that they owed more to a theatrical atmosphere than to any real world?

AA   Yes, I suppose they were slightly more stylised than later. I think, too, it takes a long time to have the courage to write people. It's not easy. You start – I started – with plot very much. It was round about the *Normans* that suddenly, because of the scale of them, I was unable to keep plotting. There was one scene that I started to write in the *Normans*, and I realised that it just had to be there because it was there; and nothing was actually going to happen in it. It was the beginning of the second act of *Living Together* when they all come in from washing up, and there was just this lagoon of peace. I had to sit down and write a play where people just sat and talked; it sounds very naive, but I'd never actually written people sitting and just chatting. I was very nervous about doing it. And I suppose out of all the *Norman Conquests* that, to me, was my big achievement, and it was that which led on to *Absent Friends*. I thought: 'Wow! I can write a play where everyone just sits down and has a talk.' Which is really what happens in *Absent Friends*: a person gets up once and pours some cream over another, but for the rest of the time they really are pretty static. You only move them round to keep the eye from getting totally bored. I'm always dismayed by people who claim that my writing hasn't moved at all since *Relatively*.

IW   Your plays clearly gain from being seen as a sequence, a development, an organism which is still growing and developing.

AA   I'm very conscious myself of using the experience of each play to go forward, and in my own mind I'm perfectly clear how it develops. In pulling one out off the shelf, as I pulled *Relatively* off the shelf to re-direct, it's a very curious experience I wouldn't want to repeat too quickly, because it's most throwing chronologically.

IW   Did you feel inclined to re-write it?

AA   Well, I either had to do that, or just close my eyes; which I did, and carried on with it, saying: 'Sorry about this.'

Schloßpark-Theater Berlin
Normans Eroberungen

Tischmanieren/Trautes Heim
Quer durch den Garten: Premiere am 13.10.76
von Alan Ayckbourn   Regie: Hans Lietzau   Bühne: Bill Dudley, Sue Plummer
Mit Carla Hagen, Uta Hallant, Lieselotte Rau, Hans-Peter Hallwachs,
Peter Matić, Jürgen Thormann   Kasse: 10-14, 18-19.30 Uhr, Tel.: 791 12 13

Annie

Sarah

Ruth

Design: Spohn Druck: Hundte

IW   You get yourself a historical perspective, I suppose.

AA   Yes. But I always describe my plays as a receding galaxy: when I've written them, they immediately shoot away and they go into a band of disfavour. Then, if they're lucky, they pass through that and come out again. But there's a certain point at which I'm really rather fed up with them, except for the wan little sickly children that one tends to keep a fond eye on. I'm rather cheesed off with *Bedroom Farce* at the moment: I've had quite enough of that.

IW   Why particularly?

AA   Oh, I don't know. I never really liked *Bedroom Farce* very much. Yes, I did: I got to like it quite a lot. I felt rather extraordinary when I wrote it, though: I didn't quite know why I'd written it. It was very strange. It cropped up in the middle of my serious phase: this rather jolly play suddenly arrived. And I think I was rather rude to it. I said to it: 'I'm an *Absent Friends* man now, a much more serious dramatist.' I always liked *Absent Friends*, but that's just blatant prejudice for a play that's had fewer productions than any other.

IW   Only in this country. All these dark Scandinavian and Teutonic countries seem to have latched on to *Absent Friends*.

AA   The extraordinary thing about the theatre in England is that the West End still, to a certain extent, is the watershed. Your play is scuppered if you don't get a particularly good showing – which I claim, sadly, *Absent Friends* didn't have. As a result it fell totally into disfavour. Three or four reps have done it, but one senses they did it because there wasn't anything else around.

   But I think I'm very lucky really. I think now I'm accepted, if not warmly congratulated, on the fact that I do have at least two separate levels that I write on. The ones that are slightly darker, in general, don't get any public and win awards. And the ones that are jolly probably get a lot more people coming to them. *Sisterly Feelings*, I hope, will get a lot of people in. I'll have to wait until I write another harrowing piece that empties a theatre in Shaftesbury Avenue before I get another award.

IW   It was 1974, wasn't it, the year of *Absent Friends* in Scarborough, that Michael Billington in *The Guardian* came out with his splendid headline about you: 'Ayckbourn is a left-wing writer using a right-wing form.' Which is directly contradictory to John Osborne's terse summing-up of Alan Ayckbourn sitting there as 'a right-wing boulevardier.' How do you react to that sort of attempt to classify you in left and right?

AA   It's all meaningless, isn't it? Of course, everyone has politics and everyone has

Poster for the Berlin production of *The Norman Conquests*

The Norman Conquests in Vancouver, Canada

attitudes to politics. I'm certainly anti-extremist; I'm very English. But again, I sit, I suspect, in the middle of most English opinion. The Tory party right wing fills me with total despair, as indeed does the Labour party left wing. I suppose the nearest I get to being political is that I'm rather attracted to things like the Social Democrats. That's the sort of area I'm after. It sounds awful, but I really like things to be fair. I think people should treat each other well. And unfortunately, in this world, it's getting more and more difficult to treat people nicely, because the suspicions are growing rather than diminishing. That is greatly sad.

IW   I think all Billington was actually meaning, when he used that phrase, was that you take the form of middle class comedy and you use it not as, say, Rattigan or Coward have done in many of their plays, to confirm the complacency of that cosy little world, but actually to question and tear apart, as often as not, the people you place within it.

AA   Yes. In trying to write a rounded character, one obviously writes quite often the very unpleasant side of them. All my characters have flaws and are pock-marked, and I don't do a cosmetic job on them. I don't honestly want to make judgements.

IW   But I do think you ask them questions which the standard light comedy writer would protect them from. And one of the techniques for doing this would seem to be, in the classic phrase of Jake Thackray, chucking a bit of grit into their life's vaseline. In quite a number of your plays, you've got this maverick character. It starts with Mint, in *Mr. Whatnot*, goes through to Tony in *The Sparrow* perhaps; even in *Ernie's Incredible Illucinations*, Ernie is creating absolute bloody chaos all round him; Leonard in *Time and Time Again*; Norman in the *Conquests*.

AA   Yes, it is a theme: it creates the conflict. And one can isolate the conflict because what one is trying to portray is normality, but you've got to have something to contrast it with, and indeed to upset it.

IW   Linked with that, the subject of many of your plays seems to revolve around destruction – I mean personal destruction in one form or another. You start examining factors within personal relationships which actually inhibit those relationships and start destroying them. Yes?

AA   Yes.

Thames Television's production of *The Norman Conquests*

IW   The destructive factors come in various forms. There's daft things like sheer social machinery: you are fascinated by mealtimes and picnics and parties and things like that.

AA   Yes, I am. Meals are convenient times when people are willy nilly forced to sit opposite each other and possibly exchange conversation.

IW   Yes, and they're crowded around with all sorts of silly little conventions.

AA   Yes – who sits at the top of the table, to start with. I'm also quite fond of extending that: there's always somebody in my plays – well, not always, but often – who wants to do things properly, according to the way they think they ought to do it. In *The Normans*, Sarah's attempt to have an embassy banquet in that naff house, with only lettuce in the fridge – it serves her right, really.

IW   She is surely protecting herself from any sort of relationship with anyone by hiding within the form.

AA   Yes, and the best thing to do is to formalise it all with everyone sitting around the table, well dressed, and having jolly conversation. And then you can be reassured that everything is normal, because the one person who is about to crash is her. She fancies Norman more than any of them, so she's fighting herself, and she's also fighting the sins of her sisters-in-law. She's really trying to touch a safe base; and the safe base is rolled napkins, and knives and forks, and man-woman-man-woman, and: 'Hasn't it been a lovely day?'

IW   The internal hierarchy of the middle class is fascinating within your plays; and the boss-employee relationship is one which recurs a bit with its sexual concomitants, which make for some really quite comical things.

AA   There's John and Paul in *Absent Friends*. Paul is John's boss and has had Evelyn. And John, who is married to Evelyn, bites his lip about it and says nothing, because he needs a contract. John's very much a parasite on the back of Paul, only Paul is himself a parasite. Big fleas have little fleas . . .

IW   In *Time and Time Again*, there's a complicated situation too.

AA   Graham and Peter: yes, indeed. In some employers – and it's American thinking, but it's come over in a half-baked way into England – the enthusiastic employer always feels he'd like to know his men as well; and by 'his men', he also means his men's women – or, if he's employing women, then his women's men. (I haven't written about a female employer

116

Family Circles at the Ernst-Deutsch Theater, Hamburg, Germany

yet: I must do that and remedy that situation. Now she is very much a prominent figure on the scene, and getting more so, that tension would be quite fascinating in reverse.) I know that I'm always interested to know quite how far employees go in some of these organisations to appease their employer. Would they actually hand their wife over? They probably would, actually, if they thought that it would help them on their way.

IW   There is in several plays an almost shadowy presence of brothers and sisters – the sibling relationship, if you like. Obviously in *Family Circles*, *Time and Time Again*, the *Normans*; there's a brother in *Sisterly Feelings* and there's a brother again in *Taking Steps*.

AA   There's a whole family in *Sisterly Feelings*. I'm very fascinated by the style of relationships there, because it is totally different from that of a chosen relationship. It is enforced, you're with someone you didn't ask to be with.

IW   You throw them together in a way which I find strange.

AA   I usually use a focal point to get them together. In the case of *Sisterly*, I've implied that Dorcas probably lives away from home for a lot of the time, but that the father, particularly now that he's lost the mother, would need visiting more. All the scenes take place at

Time and Time Again at Det Danske Teater, Copenhagen, Denmark

Time and Time Again at the Theater in der Josefstadt, Vienna, Austria

weekends, so one assumes that that's the time she comes back. And Abigail lives near – none of them actually lives with him – so that's how they're foisted together. In fact, we see them in untypical proximity, because that's the relationship I'm interested in exploring. But I find there is in many relationships – certainly parental ones, also I suspect with brothers and sisters – a sort of love-hate. There probably is a great deal of animosity, but there are moments when they just touch and react as one, because they both have the same attitude. It's a closeness that can't be touched by an outsider.

IW   The other relationship which you have foisted upon you rather than choose is the parent-child relationship, and that doesn't feature very much.

AA   Not as much as it probably will do. My own childhood is now in quite good perspective; and also, having a nineteen- and a twenty-year-old son now, that relationship is beginning to be distant enough to look back on. I'm tempted to write very soon – it was there in *Joking Apart* to a certain extent – the parents of younger children. But my great objective is never to see them: I don't want the children around at all. It's the parents I'm interested in. Then one day it would be nice to write parents with older children. That remains to be explored.

IW   The area that you've been into in enormous detail – and I suspect you're going to continue going into it in even more detail – is marriage, of course. And if anyone did a computer analysis of Ayckbourn's canon, I suspect you would end up as the greatest threat in the British theatre to Christian marriage. You really don't have any time at all for it, in the plays anyway.

AA   Well, I only write what I see.

IW   I don't believe that.

AA   Well, let's say this: the marriages I do see are either fraught or dull. There are one or two very happy ones, but that's probably because they're new. In general, I don't think people were meant to live with each other for too long – although, having said that, there are millions of exceptions. As soon as people feel that they are married, there's a sense of entrapment. That was certainly my reaction: I signed a document to say: 'I will love you for the rest of my life' – which, at that time being less than twenty, I suppose I optimistically reckoned as at least fifty-five years. I suddenly became attacked with a great sense of claustrophobia: 'My God, what have I promised?'
   But I'm less interested in marriages than I am in just man-woman relationships. Men and women are much nearer than they sometimes say they are, but at the same time they do

think quite differently and their attitudes are quite different. And it's not just hereditary or environmental pressures. Of course those are there; but even so, I am absolutely sure that, if you took two new babies and brought them up identically, you could spot their attitudes as male or female. They're just, thank God, different: I don't say there's anything better about one or the other. I suppose if they were brought up in totally equal circumstances, they would probably live very harmoniously, but they're not: they're brought up with the most extraordinary expectations. As long as we continue to make the promises we do about the opposite sex – that is to say, mostly sexual – we're going to be permanently disappointed. There aren't any page three *Sun* women, apart from on page three of the *Sun*. Nor are there those super blokes that step out of the screen: they're actually sweaty and spotty. And they're much more ordinary than that. And I think that's where the tensions come these days; it's in leading us to expect beautiful people. There are about twenty-five beautiful people.

IW   So the collapse of marriage is all to do with the collapse of fantasy, is it?

AA   I think to a certain extent, yes. I certainly went into my marriage with the most extraordinary ideas about what it was all going to be about, even though what we were setting out to do on our honeymoon wasn't a totally new experience. All the same, it was going to be marvellous. And there's a great conspiracy, because nasty old middle-aged people like oneself – I hope I don't: I've been so careful not to – gather round to perpetuate the myth. They say: 'Your mother and I have never had a cross word.' And you think: 'You lying sod, you were hitting her when the relationship mattered and it was full of passion, as it was early on, and you bothered to shout at each other. The only reason you don't shout at her now is not because you like her any better, it's that you really can't be bothered.' I think that's quite a nice state to be in, really. I don't quarrel with my relationship now, because we know all those alleyways: we've been down the shouting. In fact, I think in second relationships you can often avoid going down all those alleyways.

My biggest recurrent theme is that people do care about each other; it's just that they handle each other in boxing gloves half the time, and not with kid gloves. And I remember that all the screaming and shouting and hurling of food against walls that happened in my early relationship had to do with wanting to get closer to the person I wanted to share my life with. It wasn't that I wanted to hurt them (although occasionally I did, because I felt they were hurting me). It was to do with caring and loving: it wasn't to do with anything destructive.

IW   Yes, but your more objective self, looking at marriages within your plays, is quite clearly saying: 'Marriage is destroying these people.'

AA   I think it often is. I think a big piece of us dies in a marriage. We enter it, often spoilt, only children and in general, it goes one of two ways: we're either very bad at adjusting at all – we say: 'Yes, I don't mind marrying you, but I do object to the fact that you want this over there.' Or one personality, being stronger, will eclipse the other. Sometimes that happens by slow erosion – in the woman's case it's usually a long-term marathon: she'll just whittle away. One sees in Scarborough the man in the garden, smoking by the shed – I've seen that quite a lot – because his wife won't have tobacco smoke in the house. And you think: 'Go up to the house and say: "This is half my sodding house, and if I want to smoke a cigarette in my lounge, which I'm paying my mortgage for . . .!"' But no, he's standing by his shed having a fag because he's not allowed in the house, poor little sod. And that's a case of one personality having just gently established a superiority.

IW   Is there any sense in which you're mellowing slightly in the plays? Both in *Sisterly Feelings* and in *Suburban Strains*, you seem to come to the conclusion: 'It's not perfect, it's

Confusions at the Centar za Kulturu Novi Zagreb, Yugoslavia

not what it was supposed to be, but it's all we've got, so let's do something with it.'

AA   Yes, I am mellowing. The fire's gone out of me a bit, in that I'm no longer as indignant as I was. I was so rudely hurled into a so-called permanent relationship so early, I became very angry about the fact that nobody told us. Why should they? But now one side of me says: 'If you can get through all that fire and water . . .'; while the other side of me is saying: 'You're becoming exactly like those people who say: "You'll come through it and, you know, if you give a little and take a little, it'll be all right!"' I think, as you get older, you get a bit more tolerant. I hope so.

IW   With *Absurd Person*, even more so with *Absent Friends* and also in *Just Between Ourselves* and *Joking Apart*, you started tapping a new well. You started getting into the dark comedy, which took a lot of people by surprise at the time and still hasn't quite found an audience.

AA   Yes, the dark seam is there. I think it really came about as I began to explore the characters. As my confidence grew in holding an audience if you like. I discovered that I could start to strip the layers off the people a little bit and find, perhaps, less typical emotions than you find in your average light comedy, like anger and jealousy and fear and rage and lust: I mean real, burning, destructive desire, all those sorts of thing that one normally associates with Tennessee Williams and the swampland. Once you're into that, then obviously there are going to be some dark things, because you can't really write about it without them.

IW   By the time you get to *Joking Apart*, you've got a really very gloomy play indeed. It manages to be funny but in the process it blasts the hell out of Christian marriage, the work ethic, and several other things.

AA   I've related why I started to write it. Somebody said: 'Why don't you write about a really nice couple? I'm fed up with all these bloody awful marriages.' I said: 'Yes, I really must get this couple together.' And I suddenly realised that, in creating a happy couple – and there are people on the fringes of our lives: they're never in the centre of our lives, they're people we faintly know, which is why they're quite nebulous – they're not the central people, but they're very important to the play. I don't believe that, if we investigated Richard and Anthea beyond a certain level, we could keep up the image I wanted of them which was of perfect happiness, because it obviously doesn't exist anywhere: there must be knots. But I was interested in seeing them from our other characters' point of view. And from their point of view, as Sven says, 'Every bloody thing he touches goes right!' The misunderstanding of the play is that people often think I was writing a play about Richard

Joking Apart in Scarborough

and Anthea: I was writing a play about Sven, about us, about the inequalities of life. Why the hell should someone be born with less ability than another? Some people seem, in our lives, to have a natural aptitude for everything – everything they touch.

IW   A small point made in the play is that Richard and Anthea are living together, not married: is that particularly significant?

AA   I wanted to avoid a 'happy marriage.' I wanted to give them a grounding of less than conventionality. There's a suspicion that Anthea wasn't happy in the past, that things haven't always been that incredible: it was the mating of Richard and Anthea – a second-time-around, in fact – that fused into a sort of ideal oneness where everything came right for her. That's the only reason for that – and the fact that it gave Hugh, the vicar who destroys himself in love, a glimmer of hope. Sometimes he thinks: 'Well, if my wife dies, or she leaves me, or we get divorced, I could give up the church and I could go off with Anthea; she could leave Richard.' There's a little door with just a chink of light – awful, really.

IW   *Joking Apart* disappointed you greatly in town by the fact that it didn't run. The audiences didn't come in sufficient numbers. You went straight from that disappointment into writing *Taking Steps*, and I'm interested to know whether there was a strong element of reaction in that?

AA   I just wanted to write something fun for a change. Just as, at one point, I didn't want to be known as the king of the giggle business, I didn't want to be known as a writer who'd suddenly gone gloomy. I want to be able to write whatever I want to write. I don't ever sit down and consciously say: 'Here comes a jolly!' The company were braced for a very grim play, because they'd already realised that I wrote alternately something rather jolly and something rather dark; and *Sisterly Feelings* had been a very sunny, light, merry sort of evening – so they said: 'Hah-ha! The next one's about the axe murderer!' And, in fact, out came old *Taking Steps*, which is, in some ways, a strange mixture. It's actually quite a savage play. I always find it's much more savage than others do.
   But, this was a farce. I know Frank Marcus argues over what is a farce. He would claim *The Norman Conquests* were farces – I'd disagree with him; or *Absurd Person* – I think the second act is getting very near it. But I don't think I've written a farce for a very long time – *Bedroom Farce* certainly wasn't. *Absurd* possibly was the nearest to a black farce that I've written. And I think *Taking Steps* is a return to that momentarily. It's nice to do. Hopefully, if I get time, I shall write two or three more.

IW   Farces?

AA   Yes. I love doing them, but they're bloody hard work. They're much the hardest thing to write, and you can't do more than one every five years, simply because the technique involved is phenomenal. It's like playing a very difficult Liszt sonata: you need to have so much muscle and ingenuity. And you have to use up a stockpile: I won't have that much ingenuity again for another five years. I've got gentle ingenuity for things like *Just Between Ourselves*, but not this massive construction job that has to go on, because the more unlikely the events you wish to portray, the more credible you have to make them, and that requires an enormous amount of artifice.

IW   Your plays are translated into something like twenty-four different languages and played pretty well everywhere in the world including almost every country in the Eastern bloc. I tried to find out whether there was any record of your having been played in the USSR. I think Tom Erhardt is convinced that you've been pirated over there.

AA   Yes, you don't get many royalty cheques from the USSR.

IW   When you were doing *How The Other Half Loves* in America, I think you said you had to Americanise somewhat. Are you conscious of foreign translations of your plays having been bowdlerised in any way?

AA   There are two ways of approaching them, really, as far as I can see. They either decide to play, as we often do, say, a French farce, or a French comedy, where we carry on behaving as if French. Or we do the other thing, which is to make it into an English play. In Europe, what they do is to retain the Englishness of them. What they tend to do, I suppose, is to put all the men into bowler hats, metaphorically, because a lot of my plays confirm what they already think about England.

IW   Does that imply that they're broadening them too much, that they're caricaturing them?

AA   Not always. It's very hard to tell if you don't speak the language. I saw a production once of *Relatively,* when they seemed to play it in an orange grove: there were a lot of oranges all over the place. But that, they assumed, was an English orchard, I suppose.

IW   That was where?

AA   Berlin. Often the productions have just been lifted − the sets and the costumes and the images − from London, and they're very, very similar. But I have also seen new productions in Germany as well.

IW   Yes, the Germans are very fond of you, aren't they? They've translated virtually all your plays and play them a lot."

Absurd Person Singular at the Teatr Dramatyczny, Warsaw, Poland

AA   I've got a very good agent there, Klaus Juncker. He is always ringing up with reports of how many productions he's sold and how he's doing. It's a great challenge for him. In other countries, in Italy for example, where you haven't got that service and probably not that response for that sort of theatre, it's more difficult. But I do well in Germany and the Scandinavian countries, and Holland, too − although they all have their own peculiar problems − Spain, to a certain extent; and France, again, pretty well. The other thing that helps the plays, of course, is that my very limits are also my strengths, in that I tend to write about human relationships. And one can see quite easily in *Season's Greetings* − provided they like the play − the characters are very easy. Wherever in the world there are Christians who have Christmas − or even non-Christians who have Christmas − they have family staying with them. And it's the family coming together that the play is about. And when you have family, you possibly have an eccentric uncle and you possibly have a couple that are having a rather difficult relationship in their marriage. And so, immediately, you're nine-tenths there. What you do with the details of it − whether they all drink sherry or Manhattan cocktails − is really immaterial.

Relatively Speaking in Ljubljana, Yugoslavia

Relatively Speaking at The State Theatre, Brno, Czechoslovakia

IW Have you seen them played in Germany a lot?

AA More so than elsewhere, yes.

IW And do they get the productions about right?

AA Sometimes, not always. I have seen one, in Hamburg, which was marvellous of *Relatively*, and one of *Absurd Person* that was really very poor.

IW In what way poor?

AA *Absurd Person*? Oh, well, they played it like a jolly comedy. It had no balls to it at all. And you say: 'Oh well, they don't understand that play' — then along comes another production of it that's marvellous. But in Germany, it's the sort of theatre I rather approve of. I made the crass blunder when I first went there of asking when the production transferred to Berlin. They said: 'Berlin? You're joking! They can do their own bloody production, and it won't be as good as ours, thank you very much.'

IW Where else abroad have you seen productions of your work?

AA I've seen a Spanish production of *How The Other Half*. They're completely berserk in the Spanish theatre. It may have changed a little: I saw it during Franco. Because it's a non-union theatre, totally non-union, the hours they work are extraordinary, extraordinary. They have a second house that doesn't go up till about eleven o'clock — they do twice nightly, including Sunday — so they come down on the second house something like half-past one, two o'clock. I saw it on New Year's Eve, and they had this strange business of interrupting the play with the equivalent of Big Ben, Big Maria, which they played over the loudspeakers. The play stopped, the cast ran on, champagne was poured, streamers were thrown at the audience – a little junketing for about quarter of an hour, twenty minutes. Then, almost to the line: 'As I was saying . . .' and the play goes on again. That was very extraordinary. At the end of the show — I came on the stage for the streamers, then went off again — my translator, a nice guy called Nacho, said: 'Would you like to meet the company?' I said: 'Very much'. I came round, and they were setting up on stage with the standard sort of rehearsal furniture — chairs, tables and stuff — and moving the rest of the set back. And I said: 'Oh, tomorrow morning?' And they said: 'No, now!' So I said: 'Rehearsing now?' They said: 'Oh yes. Tomorrow the actors are doing radio in the morning, so they have to.'

IW The Dutch?

AA   It's curious: they're very short of actors, the Dutch. It's a small country. You have to book your actors. It's fascinating seeing how the different theatres run. The German theatres each have their own company of actors who are, as far as I can make out, contracted until they die; they are permanent members of that company: an extraordinary system of growing up through the ranks and taking over a part if the leading man dies. In Holland, on the other hand, which has its national theatres, its subsidised theatres, I've dealt mainly with commercial management. Commercial management has to plan its productions years ahead, just to get hold of the actors; but the shows that I've seen there have been quite good.

IW   Paris, though, played funny games with you.

AA   Yes, they played funny games with *How The Other Half*, and I got quite nasty about that. The director suddenly thought it would be nice to have an extra scene with Bob on the phone to his mother! After the play was over, the producer said: 'What do you think?' I said: 'I didn't like that scene you put in, I must say.' 'Oh, well, a little adaptation!' So I said: 'Yes, well, I don't think I'm going to let that happen any more.' One of the other strange things about it was the clothing. All those people are from different social strata: Frank and Fiona are very wealthy and they have no children, and they're successful, and he's a managing director. But Bob and Terry Phillips are struggling – they've got a young baby, and they mis-spend their money. Bob drinks a lot of it and she gives the rest to Oxfam; so they really are in quite reduced circumstances. And the whole point of the household is that she doesn't care about clothes anyway! And then Mary, in the third of the couples, is tremendously naff; and William does buy her dresses, but they're always horrible. And in the Paris production, there were three really elegant, very chic women: they looked glorious in their clothes from Dior. And I said: 'Couldn't we have them a little bit more like Mary and Terry?' And he said: 'In Paris, we do not wish to see ugly women on the stage. This is Paris.' So that was the end of that question!

Absurd Person, on the other hand, was a very good production. Ironically, they had done everything I asked – it was tough, it was real, there were no elegant, chic Evas in beautiful negligées – and it ran the shortest of any of them, because they then said: 'This is not boulevard comedy. What is it doing on the boulevard?' The people who would have enjoyed it shunned it because it was on the boulevard, and the boulevardiers backed off it because it was not jolly enough.

Relatively was another slightly strange production in Paris; they filmed the first scene. There's a curtain, and you think: 'We're going to see a play,' and you sit down. And the curtain goes up, and there's a cinema screen which says: '*Pantoufle* par Alan Ayckbourn' and all the credits. And then it starts. Everyone but me seemed to be very happy with it. Then, a marvellous *coup de théâtre*: at the end of the first scene, the girl does something and then there's a mix into a hand on a teapot; and then a track back and back and back on the

How the Other Half Loves in Hungary

camera, until slowly it encompasses first the two at the table, then the garden itself, which is palpably by now a stage set, then the proscenium arch, so that the screen fills with proscenium arch; and the screen rolls up and, damn as make any difference, there's the real scene behind. It's an amazing piece; but again, nobody seemed to take any notice. Nobody clapped or anything: it was the blasé French. The English would have been leaping around, saying: 'That's tremendous!'

IW I'm told there was a legendary production — I don't know if it ever happened — in the

States of *How The Other Half Loves.*

AA   Oh, the Gay Lib one, yes. I got a very sweet letter from this company, saying: 'We are a gay company operating in California, and we think your play *How The Other Half Loves* is marvellous. We would like to adapt it for our company, which will be, in this case, an all-male cast. And we would make Frank and Fiona, Bob and Terry, and William and Mary into gays.' So I wrote back: 'Look, you really mustn't think I'm prejudiced in any way: this is a wonderful, wonderful idea. And I think your theatre is marvellous and serves an enormous section, I'm sure, of California. But the fact is, I think you're really picking the wrong play, because there are certain central things in these relationships which are heterosexual. For instance, I suppose, just about, Frank and Fiona could be played gay, with a big pinch of salt. But certainly Bob and Terry could never be gay, because the whole action round that pair is about their baby. Terry is saying: 'I'm trapped, I'm trapped with a kid, and I can't get out. And I'm a woman with a brain.' Are you going to suggest that there is some way they have adopted a baby? It doesn't sound right: if they've adopted a baby, then they've done it voluntarily, and . . .' 'No, no, we've solved that,' they wrote back. 'We're going to make it a chimp.' So there's a man, trapped at home, looking after a chimp! I wrote back and said: 'No, I really don't think I can give my permission for this. I'm sure there must be many more plays that are more suitable. I just don't think it'll work.' So I've probably blotted my copybook.

IW   Any other foreign productions which have been hair-raising at all?

AA   Well, the American producers of *Absurd Person Singular* tried to switch the second and third acts, because audiences were laughing more at the second and they wanted to end on a high. Then there was a note from somewhere like Hungary: '*Relatively Speaking* has opened and is running very successfully now, and we're sending you royalties. P.S. The musical version is also doing very well.' We never heard any more of it.

IW   Another musical, *Jeeves*, which you did with Andrew Lloyd Webber, was not a success, but I believe you met Wodehouse.

AA   Yes. There was a sort of mooted plot afoot that it would be nice to have his approval of the show. Not a plot by Andrew and me, I hasten to add, but a plot by some managerial whizz-kids, probably up in the Stigwood Organisation somewhere. Plum lived at that time out on Long Island. He didn't have a piano, but there was a convenient young millionaire composer within a stone's throw who did. So the idea was that we'd go over to Plum's house, pick him and his wife, Ethel, up in a sort of cortège of cars and go on to this composer's house. So we arrived, and we drove through Long Island, which is very like Surrey — it gets

131

more and more like Surrey the further you go – and the first sign that we were in Wodehouse-land was that we passed a sign saying: 'The Bide-A-Wee Cats and Dogs Home,' which indeed was run by Ethel. And Ethel was, as we arrived, finishing boiling fifteen chickens for the stray dogs and cats.

IW   Ethel was his age, was she?

AA   I think she was probably about seventy; he was about ninety; so she was quite a stripling. He was very, very deaf, and he wore a deaf aid; but one suspected immediately that, like some of his characters, he wore it as a defence. He seemed to be able to hear everyone except Ethel quite well. Ethel would scream at him and he wouldn't take any notice; but you could say: 'It's a lovely morning.' 'Yes,' he'd say. Anyway, he came shuffling out. He was working on his new novel. He smiled and nodded and shook hands with us and smiled. And we got into the car and started to drive. Ethel said: 'Be careful over the bumps: he doesn't like bumps.' So we drove quite slowly, and this house turned out to be quite a long way away. Plum was muttering away in the front there about how it was lovely to be out in the open air, and said: 'Jolly good, this, jolly nice. I'd like to meet the chap who wrote the words in this. That would have been very nice.' 'HE'S SITTING BEHIND YOU, PLUM! YOU'VE JUST MET HIM! HE'S SITTING BEHIND YOU!' screamed Ethel. He said: 'Oh, he's sitting behind me? Oh, that's nice. Didn't know you'd written the words.'

Well we got there and we had our photographs taken outside. We went in, and Andrew sat down to play the score. We sat Plum by the piano, and I sat next to him to hand him the sheets of lyrics, because it was quite apparent he wasn't going to hear very much. And Andrew – I remember very clearly – put the music up, and turned round, and he went; 'Aaaah!' He looked sort of desperate. I turned round; and there were about sixty people in this room. They'd all filtered in – sort of casuals from the composer's relations and odd, very bearded, woolly Americans with Afro haircuts who were all sitting cross-legged. Suddenly, Andrew was playing a concert performance and P G Wodehouse was the last of the people to play to. The whole of the newer wave, modern American composers were there. The man who owned the place, turned out to be the foremost electronic composer. So Andrew played through the score and sang it quite well, even if he kept missing my words because he was trying to play it right. And Plum was nodding and saying: 'Jolly nice, jolly nice.' At the end of the music, our hostess had absolutely excelled herself. She'd laid on the full English tea: cucumber sandwiches, tomato sandwiches, pots of tea, scones, a full table. And Plum said: 'Ah, tea!' and absolutely beamed. And Ethel seized him by the arm and said: 'No! Time for home, Plum!' and whisked him away; and that's the last we ever saw of him.

IW   Having worked on *Jeeves*, you actually got the taste for musicals, I think.

AA Yes, but it's very difficult, I had to find someone who'd work my way. Initially, I appointed Paul Todd as the theatre's Musical Director. The writing collaboration grew from this. It soon became apparent that he works at very high speed, is extremely flexible and complies with how I'm working extremely well. For instance, we work musically to lyrics rather than lyrics to music. With *Suburban Strains*, he was the last one to know what the play was about. I would say, as it got later: 'I think we need a big I-hate-you-and-I'm-leaving-you song, something like . . .' and I'd give him a rough lyric line; and he'd bang out a melody for it. And that worked very well. Having said that, there's obviously a tremendous amount of give and take.

IW Most of the work you've done with him is in fact revue stuff, apart from *Suburban Strains*. Are you actually hankering after the great British musical?

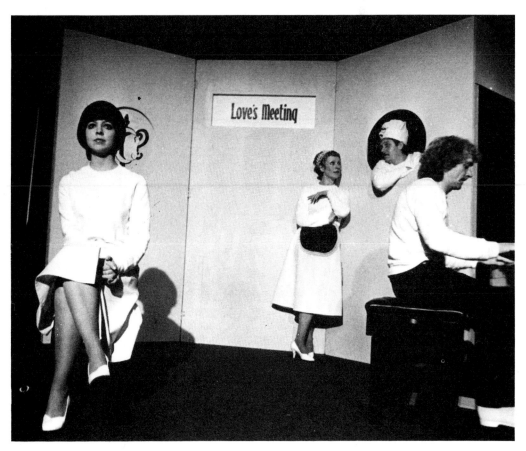

The lunchtime revue *Second Helping* at Scarborough: at the piano, composer Paul Todd

AA   No, I'm hankering after *Suburban Strains* and developing in that line. There was a very interesting development: it was only a minor one, but it's a small seed, if you like. In the second of our lunchtime shows, there were two or three songs which I call one-act songs. There was the *Fancy Meeting You* song, where the man meets the old girl friend and she says: 'I'm married now' — which is one of the more successful. There's nothing dazzlingly original about the situation, it's a miniature one-act play set to music; I've just used his music and written dialogue to it. Well, that interested me a lot, and I think we might continue writing some one-act songs. If he provided me with thirty minutes of music, the next step would be to write a one-act play on top of that. I've asked for a well-structured piece, with a developing theme; possibly a returning theme would be nice. And then I'd take that and use it as a format for writing a play round. And it'll be an opera. And then if that works, we might write a two-hour one.

IW   Music Theatre.

AA   Music Theatre. Maybe it will have dialogue interspersed, or I may come back and say: 'This tune's very successful, but I need it again, because this is the way the dramatic flow is going.' I'll try, as far as possible, not to mis-shape his images. So he's writing an overture — not an overture, it'll be more of a sort of symphonietta. And that can only work really in the sort of theatre we're at, because he's taking a lot on trust. He's turning out thirty minutes of music which could finish up on the rubbish tip, if it doesn't work. But Paul's got a great generosity of music: if you ask for a tune, he'll give you nine. Which is nice: I like that.

IW   Do you envisage music taking over your work, or just becoming another strand of it?

AA   I think it might complement it. I don't think I'll ever become a 'musical writer'. But I would like to think that if the play stream ever did dry up, that would be there. It's only when I feel I'm definitely repeating myself that I'll want to move on to another strand. But I do think the music strand is very nice: it acts as a sort of buffer. And writing songs has been like using other muscles and incidentally buffing up one's lyric writing, and actually learning a lot about it by practising it and hearing the results. And hearing the results of those twenty songs, I know the ones that I think work. You know, I could finish up being quite a good lyric writer, if I keep at it long enough; and indeed, I'm learning about music. Not about chords and notes, but about what it does to words, which is very important.

134

THE SCARBOROUGH DIMENSION

IW   On your passport, where it asks for 'Occupation', what does it say?

AA   Writer. It sounds grander on a passport.

IW   Yet you consider yourself primarily as a director rather than a writer?

AA   Yes, I do. Forty-eight weeks of the year are spent directing, or thereabouts. And really only a tiny minority of the year is spent in the physical business of writing. Directing really occupies my whole working life.

IW   And pays you nothing.

AA   No, it doesn't pay anything at all. A salary is earmarked: what I choose to do with it, or whether I choose to draw it, is up to me. Actually, I don't because I regard Scarborough as something rather special and am quite happy to refuse payment.

IW   There are two aspects of directing, and we'd better take them separately. One is being the Director of the theatre, and the other is directing shows. First of all, the theatre. Perhaps we've got to clear something up, for the history books. Everybody, as a sort of shorthand, talks about the theatre in Scarborough either as Stephen Joseph's theatre or Alan Ayckbourn's theatre. It needs to be said, I think, that had it been left simply to the pair of you, that theatre wouldn't be there; because Stephen abandoned it at one stage while he was still alive, and when he died, you were working elsewhere.

AA   Oh yes, there's a third member of the triumvirate who never gets mentioned, and that's Ken Boden. He was, I think, when Stephen first came here, Secretary of the local branch of the British Drama League. Stephen believed quite strongly that amateur theatre should be drawn into the professional theatre, and, indeed, made allies of rather quickly. So Stephen did quite a lot early on to cement our good relations with the local groups, and they've remained. And out of that, one of the people who emerged was Ken, who in time became Front-of-House Manager for the theatre. He was also – another shrewd step by

135

Stephen – a local man, and at that time an insurance agent, who sold insurance to practi-cally everyone – or attempted to – in Scarborough. He was therefore in an excellent position to welcome practically every local face that came to the theatre. So he was a very good plank in our PR drive, if you like.

Later on, in 1967 when Stephen died, Ken just picked up the reins and kept a caretaker government going until the time I started to take over in the 70s. It's quite amazing how he managed to cope at all, because one thing Stephen was, was totally unconventional. He ran the theatre as he ran theatres and as nobody else ran them, in an extraordinary robbing-from-Peter-to-save-Paul-and-back-again way. His books were idiosyncratic, to say the least. I think it's taken Ken about fifteen years even to begin to understand how a normal theatre functions. As the theatre grew, so Ken has grown with it; but the theatre he started running for Stephen, was on a totally different scale to the one we've finished up with now.

IW   Ken is actually the head of a sort of little mafia which runs the theatre, isn't he? There's Margaret, his wife, who runs the box office and there's Dorothy Ruff and Joan Gregory on front of house, who've been there, it seems, since the year dot.

AA   Yes they have; they've grown up with the theatre. And, of course, the people we've added of late, since we moved into the new theatre are Stan and Doreen Lawton. Stan is the caretaker, and he's also barman, and he's also everything else. And Doreen, his wife, does all the catering. They're another gold-plated couple; I don't know where Ken found them, but they're marvellous. And they've become a very central plank in the family. Ken's been extraordinarily successful in incorporating people like that.

IW   So in that sense, the theatre is following on a Stephen Joseph policy. In two other important ways, you're very much pursuing policies which Stephen stood for. One is the policy of having a permanent company, and the other is the policy of running effectively a theatre for new writing. The concept of the permanent company has become unfashionable. There must be very few theatres left in the country which are pursuing that policy. I think the argument against it is that, with a permanent company, you are inevitably constantly casting against the nature of the actors in the company. What's the argument for it?

AA   Well, one really ought to say first that the theatre's changed radically in one way from Stephen's. When Stephen ran the company, it was very natural that it should be a per-manent company, in the same way that, say, Hull Truck or any of those companies where the identity springs from the group, are permanent companies. We were then, I suppose, the first of the fringe theatres. And, as all fringe groups are, we were all suspect communists and suspect everything else! At that time, as an actor, you didn't mention you worked for that company if you were auditioning for another, because eyebrows went up and you could feel the black marks being added to your name; you were working with a sort of subversive.

IW   That was because it was theatre in the round, though, wasn't it?

AA   Also because it was Stephen. There was something anarchic about Stephen, and the image he gave was one of wishing to overthrow existing standards; and so, perhaps, the more conventional members of the theatre felt slightly threatened.

Anyway, establishing a company theatre, as Stephen did, was a quite normal thing to do. What's become less normal is that, as we've grown – and it really happened when we became a year-round company and got our own building – we became an established company. We became on a par, if not on a financial par, with, say York Repertory Company; and, in that sense, it became perhaps abnormal that the permanent company should continue. And that, I believe, is entirely my doing.

I believe a permanent company works, for me and for this theatre, for several reasons. Firstly, because our work – a lot of it – is original work, one needs actors with the muscle and the preparedness to tackle new work. And it isn't possible to do this with every actor: many are too slow; many actors don't react quickly enough with each other. With a new play you are asking people to do twice the work – you're asking them not only to learn the lines, but also to be prepared to test out a new, completely untried product, to take changes and alterations, and to accept a certain air of nebulousness. If you're tackling an established classic, at least you know at the back of your mind that it's going to work if you do it half well. With some of these plays you just don't know until the first night. And you really do need a sort of crack SAS team to tackle this. That's one aspect.

The other aspect is that, on the level of theatre I'm running – I mean, the financial level, where it would be impractical to expect star actors to come up – you've got to get the best actors available, and most actors feel happier and respond more readily to a company situation. It's far more interesting for them to feel a security in their working relationships, where they just respond better. And I've found that actors who've come have grown visibly under this system: their work's relaxed. Obviously, there comes a point of no return when they should leave, because their work becomes too relaxed and too easy-going, and indeed they begin to believe perhaps that they're better than they are – partly because I probably get lax enough to believe they're better than they are; and then they ought to go away and do something else. Sometimes it's six months, sometimes it's years.

It's also to do with the nature of the director I am, which is a slow one. It's probably to do with my own personality: I'm a very slow person to get to know, and to get to know people. I tend, in my first production with anyone, to let them go very much their own way. Stephen always drummed into me: don't stamp on all the initiative of an actor until you've actually seen what he can do; he's got to show you his paces. And at the end of the first show, you can say: 'Ah-ha! You're one of those actors who does this, that and the other. You're one of these actors who goes over the top on first nights. You're one of these actors with a peculiar

Alan Ayckbourn with Ben Travers, who travelled to Scarborough to see *Rookery Nook*, and to whom Alan Ayckbourn subsequently dedicated *Taking Steps*

mannerism. You're one of these actors who's downright inaudible.' And then you start to work on it, and in the second production it gets more interesting. Obviously you can't give him *no* production in the first show you do, but you give him a much laxer production; and then you begin to close in, rather like a doctor who's begun to diagnose, not only on the faults of an actor, but also on the strengths, and you attempt to build on them. And that's a long-term working relationship, and the fascination and the excitement of finding something new in someone is exactly paralleled by one's exploration of one's own writing.

IW   The other side is the audience. What has the permanent company got to offer the audience, which is where it's got to show?

AA   It's got that rather dubious side, the fact that audiences love the known. They love the known element. They miss actors when they leave. And we do try to let the organism develop with the individuals. I always say to new people coming in – and I hope it isn't a load of old cobblers that one trots out – that this is an entity which I hope is flexible enough that anyone who comes and has reasonable ideas, which can be accepted by a majority – and that's the important thing – can effectively alter the organisation and bend it. When Bob Eaton came along and joined us as a part-director, part-actor, he gave us roadshows and gave us our first bar shows. I, for my part, I think, developed his acting to an extent that he'd never developed while he was at Stoke. So he gave and we gave; and when he left the relationship had blossomed to the extent that he knew where he wanted to go from there. That's a very clear example of someone adding to the company from within it, which I hope is the way it works. And that's the value of a company. I think one's only obligation is to make sure that the thing is fluid enough, and that means constantly changing. There's always a twenty per cent addition to, and subtraction from, the company each year.

IW   Obviously a very delicate organism. What's the error rate? How many people do you employ that you regret and have to get rid of fast?

AA   Oh, there's quite a lot. Robin Herford (my Associate Director) and I go to endless trouble when we audition. I'm talking about actors particularly, and of course they are the most delicate. What you cannot tell is how an actor will socialise. You look and hope he isn't a heavy drinker; and you check with a few people, and you look at the references, but ultimately you employ him because you like the look of him and because he looks as if he can act. I have little faith in auditions, and I loathe those big workshop sessions that go on for days. It's an awful thing to say, but I tend to like people when they walk in the door. And, of course, this occasionally leads to disasters; we've had some extremely inferior actors in the company from time to time; we've had actors who've drunk; and we've had some that have been so anti-social and so unpleasant that people longed to get rid of them, because you are in fact asking people to live in each other's pockets for twelve hours a day, and in a very small concern of eight, nine actors with a communal men's, communal women's dressing room. So it is tricky, and obviously we make mistakes. You can't hope that they'll all love each other: what you can hope is that you can gather people together who, although they may well see each other's errors, respect each other as artists.

IW   A writers' theatre: there have been subtle changes over the years in the policy of presenting new writing, but Stephen Joseph's policy itself remains: that a prime purpose of the theatre company should be to present new writing and the work of new writers. There was a time – and indeed you're a product of it – when the members of the company themselves, the actors in the company, were encouraged to be the writers for it. You continued that for a time, with people like Bob Eaton, Stephen Mallatratt, Stephen Lowe and Alison Skilbeck. It doesn't seem to be happening any more: you seem to be accepting the division of labour, as it were, and commissioning writers living away from the company.

AA   Yes, it's not a conscious decision, but nor do I particularly go around asking actors if they can write. I'm obviously looking for actors primarily. Stephen often would look for writers primarily, and then ask if they could act. I don't think I can do that, because now, whereas Stephen was running at the most a thirteen-week season, I'm hoping for an actor's commitment of up to a year, maybe two years; and during that time I'm going to be putting enormous strains on that person's capabilities as an actor, because the casting is likely to be extremely wide. I can't really get by with an actor of narrow abilities, however kooky his personality is: a little charmer with one performance isn't going to last too long – it's going to get rather thin round about Christmas time! So I am looking for really a very experienced actor. As a result of asking for this level of experience, perhaps I haven't found any actor/writers. In general, although there are exceptions, the better the writer the less good they become as an actor, because they become rather like directors and like a lot of actor/directors they become more and more removed from their performance, rather detached. Certainly, as my writing improved, my acting slowly faded away. At one time I wasn't bad. I always say I'm a very bad actor, but at one time I wasn't really that bad. I certainly got worse as my writing took over.

IW   Sure, but the fact of having been an actor and having been an ASM and a Stage Manager, and a Technical Stage Manager at that, has informed your writing to such a degree that it couldn't actually have happened without it. I wonder whether the sort of writing which you're going to get from 'writers' is going to be that informed about what the theatre is. Isn't there a danger there that, because they haven't got the theatre background that you have, they rely on yours to tell them how to write for the theatre – that you work with writers in such a way as to show them how to become Alan Ayckbourn?

AA It's possible, I suppose. But I try when directing someone else's work to tackle it as a director, not as a playwright. I try and keep the two functions separate.

IW Robert Cushman, I think it was, divided current British playwrights into the domestics and the state-of-the-nations. And you were either the head, or very near the head, of the domestics. I suppose the nearest to a state-of-the-nation you've put on was *The Crucible*, which happened to be a set book – and I guess that was the motive for doing it. Does this imply that you don't approve of the other strain of writing in the British theatre at the moment? Do you not like the Brentons, the Barkers, the Snoo Wilsons, the David Edgars?

AA They're fine: I just don't want to do them myself, that's all – any more than they'd want to direct my plays.

IW Do you accept that the repertoire of the Stephen Joseph Theatre in Scarborough is actually a fairly narrow one? It's not what any other rep in the country would regard as a very balanced programme. You don't do Shakespeare, you do very little costume drama –*The Crucible* really was something out of the ordinary, wasn't it?

AA Yes. We're very limited financially. We tend to do the set book we can afford to do. And so much of our stuff's new.

IW But new in a certain mould.

AA Well, it's that way because I like it! I suppose that's what makes it narrow. I present a theatre for a community, what I think the community want to see. I also do what I think my actors want to do. And somewhere between the two, we've got to get the balance right. Our theatre's a small one; we don't have very many people; and I don't feel our resources are up to doing certain plays as well as we might. I don't see any point in us doing *King Lear*. It would be *Lear* with a lot of ASMs, and the carpenter coming on as Gloucester. It would just be awful. It seems to me that we ought to do what we do best; and undoubtedly what we do best is the domestic-scale-play – partly because the theatre is scaled that way, and partly because we are in the midst of that sort of audience. People in general seem to want to see themselves, or reflections of themselves. They want to see things that reflect their own particular dilemmas.

IW As Director of the theatre, how much of a problem would you have if you didn't have a house writer called Alan Ayckbourn?

141

Janet Dale, Robert Eaton and Christopher Godwin in *Ten Times Table* in Scarborough

AA   Oh, quite a lot, I think. It certainly helps. I'm an enormous subsidy to the theatre –not only financial, but also artistic. It allows me to take chances with other people's work, which we do. We take writers at quite early stages and take devastating risks in putting them on.

IW   Do you not worry about the time when you're going to have to find a dauphin? When Stephen went, there was a ready dauphin around, someone who was ready just to step into his shoes – or very nearly ready. What is going to happen to that theatre when it hasn't got Alan Ayckbourn?

AA   I think what'll happen is what happens anywhere: the thing will go into a period of decline. It might go on; if one were incredibly unlucky they'd just produce your plays every year so it became a sort of memorial theatre, extremely boring. But with any luck that won't happen. Theatre to me is nothing whatever to do with buildings. It's to do with the people in it, or the person in it: very often, the person. When John Neville ran Nottingham, it was sensational for that period; and it was then somewhere else's turn. Quite a lot of reps in this country are being run simply because there's a building there; and there's a group of chaps who've gone and filled it and said: 'We must do some theatre in it' instead of the other way round. In fact, they should have said: 'Look, this is the sort of theatre I want to do: now let's find somewhere to do it in.'

When I leave, there may or may not be someone of equally strong identity. I suppose ideally, if there isn't, they should close the place and say: 'You've had your theatre, Scarborough, and that's it.' And the Arts Council should bundle up their grant and look round for someone else they fancy. And it should always be a person or, better still, a group of people. It shouldn't be a building.

IW   You are rather talking about your theatre as a sort of personal fiefdom.

AA   Because I'm the nucleus of the darned thing. But having said that, rolling along as I have, I've picked up a lot of extremely talented moss, which has become more than moss: it's become a group of talents, and all I do is act as a flashing beacon, now, and attract people of like views. How long they stay, or whether they choose to branch off and become their own beacons, is up to them. But I think that's what I'm doing. Actors, in general, work best when there is a director around the place. I'm talking of me as a director now, not as a writer.

My writing is a sort of gold hook, but I hope that the actors actually like to work in the theatre because they like working with me as a director. And I think that, in terms of the theatre that I run here, I'm not bad at it. I'm less of a West End director, because I don't like the system, and I don't enjoy the way they work.

Ten Times Table at the Royal Flemish Theatre, Belgium

IW   It's fairly clear how you feed that theatre. The relationship is actually symbiotic, isn't it? You feed that theatre and that theatre feeds you. In what way does it feed you? By laying an obligation on you to produce a certain amount of work?

AA   Yes, it does that. I am very conscious that my pen is largely responsible for the theatre remaining solvent. There's got to be a play of mine floating in repertoire, or we're going to be very heavily down. And that is the main reason for writing. It also gives me the right small horizon to work for. I can't work on big horizons; I couldn't write for New York and London. I find it quite sufficient to write something to fill the space I've got; and that, I find, is quite interesting. It's interesting also to write, not for the individual members of the company, but to write for the feel that's coming off the company as a whole. It's a very nebulous thing, but, as the company changes, with new members joining it, so I get different feels – I sometimes get a very morose company, and I tend to write moroser plays.

IW   Would you have written as much had you not been director of the company?

AA   Probably not so much, because I'm very easily discouraged. I've got a terrible mixture of total confidence when attacked, and total lack of confidence when praised. The more people praise me, the more depressed I become, and the more uncertain I get of what my own work is like. And the more people go knocking it, the more confident I become that it's OK. I'm just cussed, really. I've never been, for instance, more certain that *Taking Steps* is a very good play than now the London critics have torn it up; and I'm certainly less convinced that *The Norman Conquests* ever were any good, simply because they were so over-praised that I've come to dislike them intensely. Undoubtedly there's nothing like criticism to concentrate the mind wonderfully, and indeed, you have to rally under it. And Scarborough provides me protection from too much hammer: I can simply get it produced relatively quietly.

I was thinking today about this when I was directing my new play – that what I'm actually having (and I don't see any harm in this sort of theatre) is an enormous amount of fun, creating a game, if you like, which the actors, I hope, can play with the audience. Because I want the game to be a good game and I want it to have a lot of other facets to it, I've taken a lot of care, I hope, to make it quite a deep game. But I do really treat theatre as pure art: that's why I don't like intrusions like heavy political themes. Of course one can write a play about women's liberation – it's a very important topic – but I don't think it's very satisfying when they stand on a chair and tell the men in the audience that they're pigs. And that's where I differ from agit-prop theatre, in that I hate being told things. I hated it at school and I hate it in theatres.

TEATAR *79

CENTAR ZA KULTURU NOVI ZAGREB

JUGOSLAVENSKA PRAIZVEDBA
24. TRAVNJA 1979.

režija : Damir Munitić
igraju : Ana Karić, Boris Buzančić,
Koraljka Hrs, Mustafa Nadarević i
Zvonko Torjanac

scenografija : Dinka Jeričević
kostimi : Maja Galaso

Alan Ayckbourn

design dafne perković/sitotisak atelier vrtarić

CENTAR ZA KULTURU NOVI ZAGREB
Naselje februarskih žrtava 12

IW   You're not objecting to the subject matter, you're objecting to the didacticism with which its presented.

AA   That's well put, yes.

IW   The pressure on you, then, is to produce a new piece for every season. Are you actually scared of the block, the writing block?

AA   Yes, I am. I'm worried about everything. I'm worried about repeating myself; I'm worried about the fact that the more plays I write, the narrower the options get. I've used certain things that I wouldn't want to repeat; and I am worried that there might come a time when I'm not satisfied with what I'm writing. And in that case I'll stop. The censor in me will arrive and say: 'No, this isn't good enough' – as he has arrived in the past.

IW   To what extent does the state of affairs in the Stephen Joseph Theatre affect the content of what you write? By which I mean, if the theatre is having a rough year financially, does that force you (*a*) to think of writing a smaller-cast play, and (*b*) to think of writing a more obviously commercial type of play?

AA   Well, I don't think I can do (*b*). I can do (*a*), but that happens simply because there is a smaller cast: full stop. If we're in a bad way, I'll have wound the company down by the time I'm writing. Often it's quite a problem. This time I had nine, and I was writing a play and I could only find eight! And I was saying: 'Where the hell am I going to get this other character from?'

IW   One of the slightly unusual things about your company is that once a year you go on the road and tour. What's the function of touring?

AA   It makes us money. It also – and this is the most important – gives the company a change of air, a change of audience, a change of vantage point, and, I think, a bit of an artistic re-think. The other thing is that it gives a continuity of employment, which means I can hold my actors together. They now get a month's break in the spring which they deserve and need – and nobody ever gripes about that, although, in fact, their holiday pay is only for three weeks and they have a week on the dole. And they have a two-week break in the autumn. So an actor who wishes to remain with us for a period of a year, two years, can be guaranteed continuity of employment during that time, with six weeks' break over a full year. And that's the real value of touring, because we can't yet stay in Scarborough all the time.

IW   Is there an element of not being a prophet in your own country? That is to say, if the company stays in Scarborough it's actually going to get devalued by the people of Scar-

Poster for the production of *Confusions* in Zagreb, Yugoslavia

borough; whereas if you can come back with great notices from Amsterdam, and indeed London, it's going to make them value what they've got rather more? In purely financial terms, does it help you to raise sponsorship for productions?

AA I don't think so. Scarborough's terribly unimpressed by anything that happens anywhere else. It's an amazingly insular place. Unless you've been on ITV, you really aren't very much good. And I've only been on occasionally, so I'm really not that much. People still think we're amateurs. Of course, rather like your football team, they like to check up on your away games, and they're very cross – and it's nice to see people coming to our defence – if we are, for instance, criticised by anyone nationally. The company tends to get good notices, particularly in Europe, because of course English actors are actually very good. English acting, and indeed all British theatre, is held in high esteem (it's about the only thing that is) abroad.

IW Do you consider yourself a fairly authoritarian director?

AA I don't think I'm authoritarian. I tend to suggest, and I tend to organise quite well. But I do allow actors enormous leeway. I do that because I believe that what they're likely to give me, if they've made a decision themselves, will be better than if I've made it. I resist such things as demonstrating – a thing which I hate; and I never have a play blocked when I arrive at a rehearsal: I have absolutely no idea how the moves will go.

IW You and Peter Cheeseman must be the two longest serving directors, in the same theatres, in the country. You've been in Scarborough ten years, Cheeseman's been in Stoke a little longer. Do you see yourself staying here to retirement? Or do you get itchy about it?

AA I don't see myself moving. The thing is that the theatre at the moment is flexible enough to keep me occupied. I've still got enough to explore here. I haven't got a lot of ambitions to run anything bigger, so that's out. I don't think I'd care to work freelance, because I find that inconvenient and rather boring. I like what I'm doing. It's nice working with people like we've got here. So I shall stay here. So there!

FRENETIC '80

By the end of 1979, London theatre found itself without an Ayckbourn play for almost the first time in fourteen years. At the Globe, *Ten Times Table* had made way in the spring for *Joking Apart*, which had disappointingly closed early in the autumn. Then the National Theatre production of *Bedroom Farce*, first seen in March 1977 and much re-cast since, ground finally to a halt in the Prince of Wales, to which it had been inappropriately transferred. The relative failure of *Joking Apart* clearly shook Alan Ayckbourn – and, presumably, his producer, Michael Codron; and it may well have been in part an attempt to exorcise that memory that provoked him, in 1980, into the most intensively creative year of his career. The list of his first nights in that year alone would constitute a decade in the career of most playwrights:

18 January: *Surburban Strains* (play with music by Paul Todd) at Scarborough. Director: Alan Ayckbourn.

3 June: *Sisterly Feelings* at the National Theatre, London. Directors: Alan Ayckbourn and Christopher Morahan.

8 July: *First Course* (lunch-time revue, with music by Paul Todd) at Scarborough. Director: Alan Ayckbourn.

5 August: *Second Helping* (lunch-time revue, with music by Paul Todd) at Scarborough. Director: Alan Ayckbourn.

2 September: *Taking Steps* at the Lyric Theatre, Shaftesbury Avenue, London. Director: Michael Rudman.

25 September: *Season's Greetings* at Scarborough (production transferred to the Round House, Chalk Farm, London, for a limited season, 14 October). Director: Alan Ayckbourn.

At one stage in the spring, Ayckbourn was simultaneously directing *Sisterly Feelings* at the National, directing his own company from Scarborough (though necessarily rehearsing in London) in J.B. Priestley's *Time and the Conways*, writing the songs for *First Course* and getting involved, albeit peripherally, in the early planning for the West End production of *Taking Steps*. It was in the context of such activity that the following conversations took place.

149

The National Theatre production of *Sisterly Feelings*

150

27 March: London

IW   How did *Sisterly Feelings* come to be chosen for the National Theatre?

AA   Well, Peter Hall had said, over a rather boozy evening in Birmingham (or some-where): 'You must do something in the Olivier,' because I'd said I'd rather fancy that auditorium. So when he came back after the success of *Bedroom Farce* and said: 'Let's do it again', I said: 'Give me the round one this time.' So that had been in my mind; and in fact, *Sisterly Feelings* being an open air play is suited. I hope it is. It seems to be fitting it very well, although it is a whacking space. It's enormous: you could get eight or nine of our stages on to their area. I'm running round like a maniac in a track suit just directing it.

IW   They've given you Chris Morahan as a sort of chaperone director, haven't they?

AA   When I said would I be directing it, they said yes, but I would have to have Chris Morahan, because he had experience of open stages – which I took rather amiss, but never mind. I said: 'Yes, fair enough.'

IW   Who did the casting, and, indeed, who vetted the set? I suppose that was a joint decision.

AA   I vetted the set with him. The casting is always very much a National thing, but then I quite understand that. I think it would be the same if Chris Morahan were coming to direct a play for us in Scarborough. He'd have to take the company that was there. I said who I'd like particularly, and I certainly vetoed one or two members of the company who I didn't think were right for the play; and they quite understood that and weren't difficult. There were certain actors and actresses I wanted that they couldn't take because they weren't right for three or four other plays. It was a matter of casting across repertoire.

IW   I've got a letter from you here, going back three years to when you were rehearsing *Bedroom Farce*: 'A speedy reply, as I am still holding the end of a ball of string, the other end of which is tied to the doorknob of a rehearsal room somewhere in the National Theatre labyrinth where my cast are waiting. P. Hall is really on to something, having discovered a new way of keeping a company together by designing a theatre that no-one can find their way out of.' Which seems to suggest a degree of culture shock, on moving out of Scar-borough into the National Theatre. Is it a mammothly frightening undertaking?

AA   I think it survives as a theatre despite the building rather than because of it – and I don't mean that as an architectural criticism. It's just so big. It's everything I do not stand for. But they do have, on the whole – give or take their mutinous stage crews, and the high degree of theft that goes on in any building with more than eight employees – a very super group of people in there; and I think that it's a very matey sort of building, because one works as a unit. You know, we have this 'modest' little company of some eleven actors, eleven understudies, five stage management, three directors and a few others – sound and lighting and so on: all it is is a big company within a bigger company.

IW   How do you start with a completely new company? What's the first thing you do?

AA   When you arrive? The first thing to do is that often-tried system, you read the play. That allows everyone at least to have a look at each other. This is what we did on Monday. Being a large and long play, it took us all day Monday to read it.

IW   How do you actually read *Sisterly Feelings*?

AA   We tossed the coin. Chris Morahan thought it would be rather fun, so we read the first scene, then Stephen Moore playing Simon tossed the coin, and as it happened we went straight on with Abigail. Then we left her to decide, and she decided she wanted to read the tent scene and get her bit over with; so we went through the tent scene, then read the last scene and had lunch. Then we came back. But one of the main problems of the National, as in all theatres that have eight or nine other plays in repertoire, is that you can very rarely get all the actors together. They're always about to do a bring-back, or a read-through, or a matinée, or something. We were going to lose two or three of the company after lunch, so we managed just about to get through the reading and we had to lose Michael Bryant. We read what we hadn't read in the morning.
   The next thing we did, immediately after that, was to start to talk costumes, which is always handy. Again these were things that Chris Morahan and I had talked to the designer Lindy Hemming about. In fact, Chris had made general suggestions. I'd told Lindy more practical things, like what needed to be changed very quickly, and all that business – although she'd done a lot of homework on that. Then, after the read-through, we discussed these with each actor individually, which carried on into Tuesday morning. But by about 11.45 we really had to start rehearsing, so I took a deep breath and started to block the first scene. That just meant pre-disposing the actors around the set and letting it go.

IW   Do you find at this stage that you've got some actors who are reading their way into it from a very early stage, whereas other actors are already far too far ahead and have got to be brought back?

AA   Not yet, but it will happen. I think there is a problem there and I think it's a problem for everyone including oneself. We work on a four-week cycle at Scarborough: we did *Sisterly Feelings* in six weeks, which we needed. But we've got eight weeks on it here, plus a lot of previews, and I am very aware that it could go on the boil very quickly, and then go off the boil as a result; because what they have got, I hope, is a lot of short cuts in me, in that there are far less 'ifs' if the author is directing. He cuts off a lot of avenues. I'm always painfully conscious that I don't want to cut off alternatives simply because, as an author, I don't see them, but you obviously do not let red herrings occur. But this is in effect a working company – many of them have worked together before – so I think they'll all be aware of each other's paces much more than a disparate group of actors would be.

IW   One thing you haven't said – and I'm rather surprised – is that you've sat down with your cast and discussed the play. You don't do that do you? This is a play which has got really rather an amazing gimmick. Have they not questioned that at all?

AA   No, I don't even know if half of them know quite how it works yet. I don't like to say too many broad things about plays before we start. I'm particularly painfully aware of that in a second production, where I'm obviously infiltrating things that were very successful in Scarborough, and that I don't feel too guiltily were someone else's idea – like another actor's. In general I don't use other actor's ideas, simply because they belong to the other actor, are part of him, and therefore wouldn't look good anyway. But certain little touches that you've put into a production before and obviously were working and improved a scene, you want to put in again. But if you lay them too obviously down in front of an actor, he'll reject them, simply because he feels that they must be something of someone else's. But I don't discuss, no. Certainly not a play like *Sisterly Feelings*, where I think it's better to discover.

IW   The National Theatre administration, at any rate, seems to be somewhat nervous about the gimmick of the alternative scenes. There are going to be very few performances which actually turn on the toss of a coin and the decision of an actress.

AA   One in five. The way we discussed it, there are four variations and the fifth one goes free, and that's the way they'll do it. I must say, we've had a lot of sales resistance to it, even in Scarborough, and I've settled possibly for the course of least resistance.

IW   Are you getting close to admitting that the gimmick in this play is for the benefit of the actors – or at least two actresses – rather than something which has particular appeal to audiences?

AA   It doesn't have much appeal to audiences. I think it's terrific fun for the actors. It's

THE STEPHEN JOSEPH

THEATRE IN THE ROUND

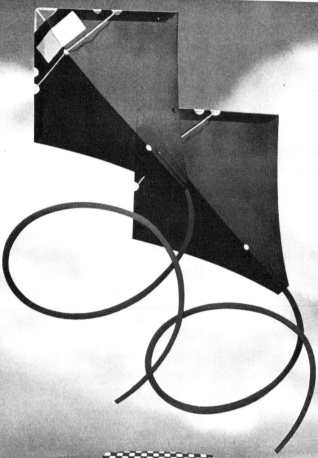

Sisterly Feelings

A related comedy by Alan Ayckbourn

With financial support from Midland Bank

The Stephen Joseph
Theatre in the Round
Valley Bridge Parade
Scarborough

Mon	4 June	7.45	Wed	4 July	7.45	Fri	20 July	7.45	Thu	23 Aug	7.45	Sat	8 Sept	7.45
Tue	5 June	7.45	Thu	12 July	7.45	Sat	21 July	7.45	Fri	24 Aug	7.45	Mon	10 Sept	7.45
Wed	6 June	7.45	Fri	13 July	7.45	Thu	2 Aug	7.45	Sat	25 Aug	7.45	Tue	11 Sept	7.45
Thu	28 June	7.45	Sat	14 July	7.45	Fri	3 Aug	7.45	Mon	27 Aug	7.45	Wed	12 Sept	7.45
Fri	29 June	7.45	Mon	16 July	7.45	Sat	4 Aug	7.45	Tue	28 Aug	7.45	Thu	20 Sept	7.45
Sat	30 June	7.45	Tue	17 July	7.45	Mon	6 Aug	7.45	Wed	29 Aug	7.45	Fri	21 Sept	7.45
Mon	2 July	7.45	Wed	18 July	7.45	Tue	7 Aug	7.45	Thu	6 Sept	7.45	Sat	22 Sept	7.45 (last perf)
Tue	3 July	7.45	Thu	19 July	7.45	Wed	8 Aug	7.45	Fri	7 Sept	7.45			

very difficult to describe: I'm absolutely sure – and the company in Scarborough would swear to it – that the free nights had a *frisson* which was not there on a fixed night. And indeed, often on the chance night, the night where one never knew, the response was better.

IW   Doesn't it put a particular stress on one actress, or on one of two actresses, who might actually act out of spite against the rest of the company?

AA   They've got to like each other, that's always been a prime pre-requisite!

IW   I've never worked out what the play finally says. It questions the quality of decisions and the arbitrariness of decisions.

AA   It came out of giving too many interviews really, where one tends to put together a group of facts conveniently. You know, I would say: 'Then I decided to leave Oxford Playhouse and go back to Scarborough, to write plays.' I didn't decide any of those things really: the season finished, and this happened or that happened. Circumstances did it, and it was only afterwards that one put on the decision-making process. That's what it's saying, in fact. The other thing I suppose it says is that it doesn't make all that much bloody difference anyway. Unlike a lot of plays which say you always get married to the wrong person, it also says that you always get married to the right person: if you don't like them, it's probably your fault for being the sort of person you are. You've got the person you deserve. I think Abigail has Patrick because she needs Patrick; and Patrick does for her what a big, glorious, bronzed idiot can get nowhere near doing for her.

IW   At what stage will you leave rehearsals?

AA   I don't think I need to leave rehearsals that much. In the last couple of weeks or so, I start rehearsing the Scarborough company, but I'm hoping that, with the National schedules going the way they are, I can actually do both without any problem. I can rehearse Scarborough in the evening, you see. The National have so many other commitments that I guess I'll do one period with the National and two with Scarborough.

IW   Will you still be working on it during previews?

AA   Oh, I think we'll have to. With an experienced cast like this it won't be that much, but there's always a certain five-per-cent of ideas in a production about which you say: 'Well, it was a good try, wasn't it?'

IW   And after previews it's freeze-dried and left as it is, is it? What happens if they re-cast? Do they bring you back in for that?

Poster for the Scarborough production of *Sisterly Feelings*

AA The National have a very efficient system. We have a staff director called Kenneth Mackintosh, who is sitting in rehearsal. Chris Morahan said to me: 'Wouldn't it be awful to be one of those directors like Peter Brook, or Samuel Beckett, and to have somebody writing down everything you say to actors?' A voice behind us said: 'I'm writing down *everything* you say to actors' – and it was Kenneth Mackintosh. He said: 'It's very handy, because when it comes to an understudy or to a bring-back, and neither of you is here, I have got everything you've ever said about that character; and I can sit down with an actor and I don't just say: "Old Fred used to do this", but I can actually say: "The reason he did this was because we talked about it, and this was said and that was said" – and the actor knows the whole background.'

IW You mention understudies. What do you do with understudies at this stage of rehearsal?

AA Well, it was a dilemma on *Bedroom Farce*. The National has a great number, and they say they're very necessary. They have far more understudies than, say, the West End does.

IW They have small parts in other plays? So they don't have this terrible thing of being life's understudies?

AA They do have bits and pieces. I'm afraid there *is* a core of actors at the National who are desperately underemployed, and who do the odd Platform shows and things like that, which are obviously nice for them. But a lot of them that I've spoken to have gone quietly nuts, sitting around hoping that their moment will come. With notable exceptions – and there are always one or two – those big theatres, the National and the Royal Shakespeare, are not worth . . . well, I don't say they're not worth joining, but, if you join them on a certain level, on that level you will stay. If you join them as a good, solid, support actor, you *may* finish up playing King Lear, but you're likely to remain a good, solid, support actor. If you join on the understudy level, you'll get valuable experience watching Paul Scofield from the back, but you're not going to finish up playing the lead, because they're going to be plucking in interesting actors from outside to do that. Michael Stroud got to play in *Bedroom Farce*, and he was the understudy; but I think he didn't expect to finish up on Broadway. It was a lovely chance for him. Two or three of the understudies on *Bedroom Farce* wrote and said; 'Please, what do I do?' I wrote and said: 'If you really want to act as much as you say you do, you'd better leave and get yourself a job in a less grand company, where you can do your Hedda Gabler.'

IW Which gets me back to my question originally: what do you do with them at this stage of rehearsal? Do they just sit around?

AA They sit around, they follow their principal, try to listen to all the notes he's got. I try, after that, to get rid of them a bit, because they tend to form an audience. I know in *Bedroom Farce* – I've noticed in this one they're very, very quiet: it's probably as a result of my complaint – they were a lovely bunch, but every time there was anything funny, they laughed. Now that's super, the actors loved it. But as Michael Kitchen said, the second time he did it, he didn't get such a good laugh, because they'd seen it; and the fifteenth time he did it, he didn't get a laugh at all. What happened then, said Michael, was that he began to push the business up to get the laugh back again. And so he was playing artificially because an actor of any sort plays to anything that's there – you play to the cleaners. So I said to them: 'Could you shut up?' And they all sat there looking miserable and feeling terribly unwanted, and I said: 'I didn't mean that, I really didn't. I just meant that if you do this – if you encourage the animals – they'll perform.'

IW And do you ever get to rehearse the understudies?

AA No. They're very rarely directed. I think there are one or two wonderful directors who do, and Chris Morahan may well take them when I've gone, but I don't think I will ever see them. In general, in the West End, the understudies would never expect you to. The Company Manager would normally direct them. But I do think that, in terms of under-studies, the West End is a particularly ill-prepared place. The National is probably, in my view, a little over-prepared, although I think it's a fault in the right direction. But it's also extremely expensive.

IW What do you do in Scarborough if someone's ill? Or do you just pay them not to be ill?

AA It's slightly different there. We play in repertoire so we usually have another show available. It did happen once and we changed the show. We said: 'Sorry folks, we can't do it. We're going to do another one, and anybody who has seen this show can have their money back.' Twenty per cent of them had their money back, the rest came in and we said: 'Apologies, this is it. We can hardly remember this show: we've all just run round and got the props.' And we did it, and people said: 'It's the best show we've ever seen.' Oh God! So much for rehearsal! No: we have a small coverage, in that we've usually got an overlap actor or actress in the town and we can survive; but it's a little different in a company like that than it is in the the West End, where you pull up in your taxi and go to see Glenda Jackson . . .

9 April: London

IW When we last spoke, you were three or four days into rehearsal: you're now into your third week. How is it working out between you and Chris Morahan?

AA He's still shadowing me very closely. He's been taking people off into the smaller rehearsal room when there's been a chance, and working with them, talking through the parts in some detail. One of the odd things about taking on a company like this is getting used to their work patterns. My work patterns are much more fragmentary: I like to stop much more frequently. The National Theatre actually don't – it's like trying to stop a great machine, trying to stop them. I think if you left them, they would run scenes all day. I like to bounce in and interrupt, and there's always a feeling of 'Oops, we've got to stop again!' I think probably Chris is the sort of director who allows the scene to run, makes his observations and then runs it again – a sort of technique which I believe was used by people like Max Reinhardt – whereas I am the jumper-in and interruptor extraordinary, in the early stages, and rather wary about letting the scene come together until later. But there's no hassle: I'm adjusting to that style.

  I'm glad he is there. He's taking so much of the weight away. He's talking to them about the kite for example. We worked out where the kite will fly, roughly, and he's now working out the flying system for it and talking about that – quite apart from being in rehearsal. He's also transmitting information day by day and being an extremely effective production administrator, as well as putting in his four-ha'porth of notes about the scenes: they tend to be more general, and he feeds back his overall impression of the scene.

IW Out of rehearsal, do you get involved in the publicity machine? Does Alan Ayres come in with graphics suggestions from the publicity department, for example?

AA We had a meeting last week, mainly about programmes and posters in which we met their department. We discussed the contents of the programme: they were very anxious that a person coming to the show would know *(a)* what they've seen and *(b)* what they've missed, so that they can choose to see another one. I suggested that if they chose rather carefully they could actually tell the story in the programme in pictures, so that the audience could recognise what they'd seen; and it would be more interesting than a long blurb. We're taking a couple of ideas from Scarborough: we're going to have a family tree instead of a cast list, and we're also having some holiday snaps. By the end we'd decided on a programme smaller in size, but thicker, because in fact we'd got so many ideas going. And they did respond, that's the good thing.

29 April: London

IW When I last spoke to you, rehearsals seemed to be very warm and friendly and tension-free. Is that still the case? Are they going well?

AA They are going well: I think I'm not living in a sort of cloud-cuckooland. The big problem's been, as I said at the outset, the timing of it. After this week we have a fortnight, from Monday, still to rehearse, and then we go into the theatre and the technicals start, and the previews start at the end of that week. So we're getting within a stone's throw. I'm gently beginning to accelerate. We'll probably finish this week with a couple of run-throughs. We've been into the Olivier for two days, and we managed to run both combinations.

IW   It's the first time you've been into the Olivier, is it? You've been in the rehearsal room.

AA   We've been in rehearsal room all the time. We're on the *Othello* set, one of the most depressing sets I've ever been on – I mean, for my play. It's very dark and black. I said: 'I'll give a small prize for anyone who can get a laugh on this set!' But it was a very useful exercise to be in the Olivier. It's a big theatre and I have never worked in it, so it was very important I saw the play. Actually, I think my instinctive blocking of it, give or take the odd move, worked. The thing one's got to adjust is some of the scale of playing. The ideal position for most actors in my plays is about six inches apart, talking in low whispers. We compromise slightly in Scarborough by putting them two feet apart, talking in slightly raised voices; more so in the pros arches around the country, where they're often standing four feet apart, talking quite loudly. In the Olivier, you have to stand about eight feet apart and shout. I'm sure it works for epic drama, but I think modern plays will continue to have problems with it.

IW   You specifically chose to put the play in there, though, didn't you? What possessed you to do that?

AA   I didn't like the Lyttelton very much. I think the theatre that I probably would have loved best, but it's completely impractical, is the Cottesloe. It's much more suited to me than either of those big ones. But I'd love to conquer the Olivier. I think it *is* possible to do a modern play there and I think it *is* possible to do a modern comedy there, but I do think it does present enormous problems. It's a problem of focus really. I think you either go in the round and you don't have any focus – except that the focus is the stage – or you're in the pros and the focus is very clear. In the Olivier, the actors are a little uncertain as to which way they're supposed to play. And, of course, a lot of problems of theatres like that come back to the root one of delivery: if you're an actor who is old-fashioned enough to sound the ends of your words and your d's and t's and have very, very good delivery, there is no problem. It's perhaps our modern school of sub-quasi-natural telly artists who tend to like to mutter a bit and throw it all away.

IW   But they're going to have problems in any big theatre, aren't they?

AA   Yes, they are. But it's a difficult theatre. I've seen the set spread over quarter of an acre of workshops, all in little bits, and it looks enormous. What it'll look like when it's all together, and lit, and in that space, heaven knows. I hope it won't draw from the actors to the extent where you're just aware of a lot of grass with some ants moving around on it. It is an amazingly complex piece of building. I was most impressed looking at the sort of fretworkery. It's a steel base, on the higher levels, and then a wooden structure with very carefully fretted, contoured pieces on a rigid forma, covered again with a cross-structure of latticework of soft-ply, covered again with a canvas material, which is glued, so it makes a very solid, but springy, base, covered by acres of green carpet, which has been laid down, and then certain portions of it have been shaved or cut. That again is covered, some of it with plaster, which creates cart-track effects and mud. And the whole thing is then sprayed. At the moment it's a sort of olivey green, but eventually it'll be eighty-eight different shades of green, as much as Alan Tagg and his spray gun can manage.

I had an eye-opener, just going round. The workshops, for instance: there's two huge rooms with a vast crew working. I then went into the prop shop, which is rather like one of those Victorian places where you saw the girls making bonnets. There are seven or eight people sitting around a huge table, all stitching leaves and plants. We're employing about twenty-four people out the back there, a little industry, just making *Sisterly Feelings*. Tomorrow, they'll be making something else. And suddenly you realise the scale of the operation: it's vast. This is a very big theatre.

IW   You're very much geared to a nine-to-five existence there, aren't you?

AA   Yes, they're very, very careful not to run into overtime. I think that's one of the big reasons for their eight-week rehearsal period. And fair enough: one accepts that. I'd imagine that, if you once started to let that floodgate open, it would be phenomenal: an actor can double his salary very, very swiftly, just on a few hours' overtime. In the National, God knows, it would be astronomic.

IW   You were afraid at the outset that, by about this stage, which is five weeks into rehearsal, you were going to be getting one or two people giving performances rather than rehearsals already. Is that happening?

AA   No. In fact, the pace of work has been far, far slower. I think the actors have realised the potential danger, and I have very consciously been refusing to allow the play to come together. I'm deliberately fragmenting it still, allowing little bits of it to come together and then go apart again, so the actors are still working in detail rather than in general terms.

IW   May we go back to the problem of re-casting. Did you actually see – whatever it was – the third, fourth or fifth cast which was playing in *Bedroom Farce* in London, still under the banner of the National Theatre, but obviously with a cast, none of whom had been through the whole period of rehearsal that you'd taken?

AA   I saw one version, and I was very disturbed by the way the show had shifted from what it originally was. And I made my views very clear to the National about that. It's one of the reasons that I'm not directing *Sisterly Feelings* on my own.

Michael Gough and Joan Hickson in the National Theatre production of *Bedroom Farce*

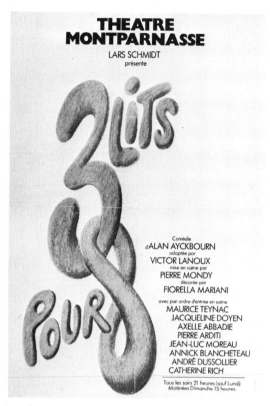

Two posters for *Bedroom Farce*: left in New York, right in Paris

IW   Can you characterise at all what went wrong with *Bedroom Farce*? You say you were disturbed by it. What actually were you disturbed by?

AA   I don't altogether blame the company. I think that one of the huge problems the National always faces is where to take its shows – there are only about eight theatres in England that will actually accept sets of the scale the National build them on: the Lyttelton's an enormous stage. The Prince of Wales was the only one that was free. It certainly isn't a theatre that you would normally expect to see a straight play at. I think the combination of being at the Prince of Wales, where you would expect to see revue or something fairly light – even strip – and being a thing called *Bedroom Farce*, together gave it an audience which wasn't actually right. They said on Saturday nights it was hell; it was full of the Navy, screaming and whistling and shouting: 'Get 'em off!'

Now coming out of the rather cosy cocoon of the Lyttelton – where you've got a discerning, American-intellectual, Surrey audience laughing heartily at all the nuances of

Bedroom Farce in Athens, Greece

the Home Counties – into this sort of Portsmouth reunion party, I think the show deterio-rated rapidly, into something coarser than it should have been. Some of the performances were amazingly broad. And I think an actor will attempt desperately to adjust his per-formance to what he thinks the audience is looking for. Certainly, when I saw it, they were playing very carefully to the gallery, and, the original cast having gone, there was no tradition to maintain it and it was a very crude affair. I was very shocked and upset, but having not been there to supervise it, and understanding fully what they were going through, I wasn't in a position to say very much.

Bedroom Farce produced by the Australian Elizabethan Theatre Trust, Sydney, Australia

IW   Getting back to *Sisterly Feelings*, one difference that struck me between your working in Scarborough and your working in town is that in Scarborough you work not only with a company which is used to working together, but with actors who are roughly of an age – they're all fairly young. Here you've got a really wide range of ages, haven't you? Is there any age tension at all between them, or do they gel together? Or do you have any problem pacing rehearsals to take account of the different ages?

AA   It's a strange feeling, actually. They seem to be, as people, extremely friendly. I suppose it's a room full of very happy, nice people, all of whom seem to like each other and respect each other's work. I sense it's less of a company than I'm used to, possibly because the actors are that much more advanced on their careers and thus that much more careful of their own little area. I'm used in Scarborough to indicating an area, and leaving the actors to work it out. This company tends to hold back from that. But I think that is partly because, although they are a company, they won't necessarily have worked in this combination. I think that the willingness is there, but the experience isn't.

IW   The state of rehearsals now: are you and Chris Morahan working separately, or are you both sitting in the same rehearsals?

AA   We've only split occasionally. We're certainly together now. He's adding his notes where he wants to and I'm grinding on. This week I'm working through every scene. I think we'll have done every scene and we'll finish up at the end of the week with two run throughs. The same next week: I shall bash away just trying to iron out the snags. They're getting smaller, the difficult areas: today we ran both second scenes, and you can almost draw little blue circles round the bits. You go 'Whoops! We must sort that one out.'

IW   Taking stock of your life at the moment, we've got you directing *Sisterly Feelings* at the National Theatre. Any minute now, on top of directing at the National, you're going to be coming off in the evenings and directing your season for Scarborough. At the same time as all that, you're writing two lunch-time shows for Scarborough. You are scheduled to write a new full-length play for Scarborough, to go into rehearsal at the beginning of September. And, whilst I don't suppose it's going to take up much of your time, *Taking Steps* is going into the West End in the autumn, directed by Michael Rudman. Don't you ever get somewhat tired with all that hanging over you at one time?

AA   Yes, I think I tend to get a bit greedy: I mean, eyes-bigger-than-the-stomach time. I enjoy a hard workload. Part of it's inevitable. I don't think I'd have chosen, if I'd had my way, to have rehearsed Scarborough simultaneously with the National Theatre. I'd love to

Bedroom Farce at Den Nationale Scene, Bergen, Norway

have finished with *Sisterly Feelings* and *then* started *Time and the Conways*. I can write simultaneously – that's no problem, certainly the scale of stuff I'm doing for the lunch-times.

IW   That's the one I would have thought was the most tension-giving, insofar as it's totally creative: you start with a blank piece of paper and you've got to create.

AA   If I am writing an original full-length play, I've got to have total quiet. This is likely to be mainly lyric writing, which I find can be contained within a couple of hours. I'm not saying that the couple of hours aren't bloody hard work, but, as it were, you can see the end of a song, and you can say: 'OK, I'm going to tackle this song tonight.'

IW   But don't you ever sweat over a word?

AA   Oh yes. The songs in *Suburban Strains*, some of them, took a day, a hard day. But some took twenty minutes, you know: suddenly it all happens. With these, I hope, I'll settle down and be able to work on them: it's the sort of thing you can leave, like a jigsaw puzzle, unlike a play.

IW   When actually do you do your writing, if you're directing ten till six and eight till midnight?

AA   Well, in between times, you know.

IW   There aren't any times in between!

AA   Lunch-time! I don't know!

13 September, Scarborough

IW   We last talked about three weeks before *Sisterly Feelings* opened, and it looked a bit like a birthday party with everybody having a lovely time. Did you have any last-minute crises?

AA   We didn't really have any crises. I think I experienced a very odd sensation because I actually gently withdrew from the production at the very point when I would be expected to be most involved in it. I began to start rehearsing *Time and the Conways*, for the first week down in Parson's Green, which meant commuting. I did a morning with the Scarborough actors, an afternoon with the National actors, and then back again to Parson's Green for an evening with the Scarborough actors. And that went on for a week, and then somebody brightly suggested: 'Why don't you have a rehearsal room in the National?' – which I'd never thought of. And at the National, because we were at this point moving up into the theatre, there was a rehearsal room free. So we brought the Scarborough company into the National Theatre, which was very nice.

But by the time we were doing really big technical dresses in the Olivier proper, I was very little involved. I was quite glad in one sense to leave it to Chris, except that it was a little annoying, because I'd bounce in and say: 'Well, no, I don't like that car tape. Can we replace that?' The sound men would look rather annoyed because they'd got it all to Chris's specification but not to mine. But they coped. And, of course, I saw the first four or five previews, but then I didn't even see the opening, because I'd gone back to Scarborough; in fact we opened *Time and the Conways* the very same night that they opened.

IW   Were you generally satisfied with the reception *Sisterly Feelings* got?

AA   Yes, I was quite pleased. Looking at them for a second time, I was fairly critical of them as plays. I can see the flaws in them very clearly, more so perhaps than in other plays. And I've always apologised for the publicity that said you should see them four times.

Having said that, I think they do hold up. There are some delightful performances in them. What I liked about them was just the atmosphere that came off the Olivier. The set was wonderful and I think the rainstorm, and the things like that, were magic. On the whole one got roughly a deserved reception for them – sort of favourable with a quota of reservations.

IW   Is your relationship with the National in cold storage now?

AA   It's very cordial. When I left, Peter Hall said: 'I do want you to come back, maybe 1981. Could we think of the 1981 play' – that's my next one – 'as being a National play?'

IW   Which would mean 1982-3 in town.

AA   Yes, it would be then. He said that, by then, *Sisterly* will have been out for about nine months – you know, a decent pause before the cries of outrage as yet another of mine goes in.

IW   Since *Sisterly* things have been going berserk, haven't they? You've written and directed two lunch-time shows for Scarborough.

AA   Yes, I'd been writing the songs for *First Course* while I'd been at the National, writing a song every few days. Actually, one doesn't realise it, but a forty-five-minute lunch-time means ten songs! And so I really had to do ten songs for the other half of the company, otherwise there'd have been some sort of 'unfair' feeling. So I sat down as soon as the first had opened and started to write the second one. That was much bigger than I thought it was going to be. Enjoyable feeling, but twenty songs is rather a lot. And then it was time to work on what turned out to be *Seasons' Greetings*.

IW   As a seasoned watcher for white smoke coming out of the chimney, it did seem that *Season's Greetings* was causing you a bit more bother than usual. Whatever happened to *Sight Unseen* (as it was originally announced)?

AA   I was going to write a thriller. I like thrillers, I really enjoy reading them, and I quite like whodunnit plays. But if you're going to write a good whodunnit, everyone's got to have done it, you see; and you then pull away about six motives and leave one there. And then you say: 'Ah yes, he's the one who did it, because he was the only one who had the front door key.' But the point is that I first of all had to write a cast of homicidal maniacs, because they all had to have killed Mr.X. And that was extremely boring. When you've got a couple of homicidal maniacs it's quite fun, but here they were all saying: 'I really hated him, I'd have killed him if I'd had the chance.' And I felt there were awful limits in having to prescribe your characters' behaviours. I'm very used to letting my characters roam around much more freely than that. To have to saddle them with a load of hatred and malice, or even sheer clumsiness, was very hard. And I didn't want to write a straight whodunnit where we just eliminated it down to one: I wanted to write a whodunnit where any one of them could have done it – to keep it absolutely open. And I came to the conclusion it was rather a boring thing to write.

IW   Did you start writing it?

AA   I started writing it, but it was so boring. None of the characters would come off the page.

IW   How long were you actually writing this before you scrapped it? How far had you got?

AA   Well, it's wrong to say I was actually into the dialogue stage. I was into the construction stage: I was putting up the fences. I then did a *volte face* and left myself with just two things from the thriller. One was that I set it in a hallway which I quite liked, and which meant I had half a dining room and half a sitting room, so that I could wander people across the sitting room to put out their cigarette, or whatever, and they disappeared off stage – those rooms were sort of shadows. A hall is an interesting room because people are always passing through it on their way to something else. I also left it at Christmas, which is an area I have visited before, but never quite as a family Christmas: before it was the Hopcroft's-in-their-kitchen Christmas. And I went back to what I've been trying to write for quite a long time – which is a love story.

IW   Is it a comedy, a play, a drama?

AA   It's a comedy. It's somewhere between the *Normans* and *Just Between Ourselves*.

IW   What is the worst that happens to anyone in it?

AA   They get shot. There's a love story that goes wrong. And there's a puppet show, which I've always wanted to have in. The house is running with kids: we never see them of course, but they're always around. One of the characters is obsessed with his annual puppet show: he writes from September onwards and makes the puppets, and every year does it on Boxing Day. All the other adults, and the kids, are trying to stop him, because these shows are the longest, most boring experiences. The year before, we learn, he did *Ali Baba and the Forty Thieves*, which went on most of the night. This year it's *The Three Little Pigs*, which sounds better, but . . .

It's based on my experiences at Christmas. My younger son used to have a puppet show, and I used to come home two days before Christmas, write the script, and get it on. But it was desperately serious and there was no fun to be had anywhere. There was a full technical rehearsal, with a lot of screaming and tears, and: 'Get that dog on the stage!' and: 'That scene change has got to get some time off it!' It was only done for Grandad and Granny, but the work that went into it was wonderful. And puppeteers are very funny: they're quite often hysterical, possessive people who fight a lot. So that's in there, too.

IW   The basic relationship in the play is a love relationship?

AA   It's a strange relationship. There are the hosts, Belinda and her husband who's called Neville. Belinda's getting a sort of five-year itch and she's feeling a bit neglected – nothing serious. And her sister Rachel, the older and less eye-catching one of the pair, who is really getting a little bit old-maidish – though actually there's nothing frumpy about her – brings down a writer (the first time I've had a writer!). And Belinda and he just go da-doi-ing! as soon as he comes in the door. What Rachel wants from him is a friendship. And it's a sad thing, really, because it seems that you can't have that sort of friendship with a man like Clive. Her sister, who's just bored over Christmas, can have a deeper relationship with him in two seconds underneath the Christmas tree, which she does. In the end, Rachel sort of gets him back, but we all know it's not going to be for long. The next time Clive meets somebody in a theatre queue or somewhere, he'll be off again.

Season's Greetings at Scarborough

IW   You end on a minor chord?

AA   Yes, all the plays end on minor chords – well, most of them – it's a wry play.

IW   You're doing something rather strange with this. You're playing it in Scarborough for four days, then taking it straight into London, in the Scarborough production, to the Roundhouse.

AA   Yes, that's terribly Russian-roulettish.

IW   Very Russian-roulettish, and does it not also foul up any chance of it going into the West End at a later stage, in a West End production?

AA   The mood I'm in at the moment, I don't really mind. It is likely that a play that's been rehearsed by me here with my company, and played for four performances, and taken down there and done pretty roughly in the same format, is likely to be as good as anything that's

171

done without me by a different set of actors, and rehearsed for a different sort of theatre. I feel the play will be seen fairly. Somebody wrote in *The Stage* that perhaps one ought to think of London as almost just another touring date, as far as the regions are concerned. I'm beginning to feel a bit like that. We're taking *Suburban Strains* down in the spring for six weeks, and that'll be its London run. There's no way that's going on anywhere else. It'll be seen and if anybody wants to do it, it's there. If they don't, then we'll take it away. That's it.

IW   At the moment, you must be feeling fairly shell-shocked, I would think. You've had one hell of a year, creatively and productively. Is your life still scheduled ahead? When do you reckon to get your head down again?

AA   To write? We've had such fun with those lunch-time shows, we might write a little tiddly thing. But I won't actually write again, I think, a serious play until this time next year. *Suburban Strains* was an interruption to the thing: it was another play which stepped the pace up quite a lot. It was like putting an extra beat into the bar.

IW   Provoking the editor of *The Stage* to suggest that perhaps you're being too prolific for your own good.

AA   Ah well, yes. Well, as Peter Hall nicely said to me once: 'If you didn't write so much, they'd realise you were quite good.' If you write too much, you can't be any bloody good!

IW   You're stocking up nicely for the post mortems, really, aren't you? Once you're dead, they'll go back to them and find . . .

AA   Like Jim Reeves records! A string of posthumous plays!

IW   Or like Buddy Holly, they'll suddenly discover . . .

AA   Oh marvellous, they're still releasing them, aren't they?

IW   And have you got the thriller right out of your system now? Or is it back on the shelf – perhapsville? You've been talking about this for so long, and now . . .

AA   Sorry about that. Yes, I'm disappointed about that. I don't know, I don't think I'll write that. I'm still after my two-hander.

IW   And how about your two-floorer as well? That's still there, is it?

AA   Oh yes. Well, I suppose so. Of course *Taking Steps* rather cut into that, but I did it without the stairs. It's very interesting: it's the first time that a play of mine – *Taking Steps* – opened in London while it was still running in Scarborough. I've never done that before. It was like looking at two pictures. And you say: 'Well, I don't care what they say down there and whether they think this or that. There's a whole group of people in here who are having a whoopee – they're having a marvellous time.' And in that sense one was perhaps able to survive the buffets of that experience better.

IW   You said about *Absent Friends*, though, that once a play has been less than successful in London, it sort of dies, because the reps are not that keen to pick it up. OK, *Absent Friends* is just beginning to pick up now.

AA   Maybe that's what I mean: it sort of dies, but maybe it just gets partially buried and they dig it up. And then somebody's very pleased when they re-discover it. God knows what plays will actually survive one, if any. They'll probably be absolutely amazing. Good Lord, when you're actually remembered just for *Absent Friends* . . ! ('He wrote a lot of others, you know!') Or perhaps none at all. But, as for *Taking Steps*: because a play remains on the page, someone, sometime will dig it up; sometime, someone will do it very well. And if they don't, I might, if I'm still around. In the same way, I suppose, *How The Other Half Loves* should have died. It palpably was just a vehicle for Robert Morley; but it survived longer than, say, with respect, *Halfway up a Tree*, which doesn't seem to be around too much – which was also a vehicle used by Robert Morley. So I suppose one could say that if the play's strong enough, it'll somehow survive.

   A woman wrote to me when *Bedroom Farce* was at the Prince of Wales, at its lowest ebb, with the eighteenth cast change, who hadn't seen the director for eight months. She wrote, absolutely outraged, and said she'd never had such a rotten evening in the theatre, and the publicity was a con and she felt like suing. She lives in Kent, and she wrote to say: 'I must tell you that the Marlowe Theatre, Canterbury, decided to do *Bedroom Farce*, and I and my husband, who'd already suffered it, with great reservations went along again to see it.' And she said: 'It was marvellous, just wonderful. And it just goes to show,' she said, 'we didn't realise how a performance can alter a play. Marvellous! So now we want to see all your other plays.' The irony was that the Prince of Wales production was mine!

THE SQUARE CAT (1959)

Father, son and daughter are perturbed to discover that mother has developed an obsessive passion (from afar) for a teenage pop star, and even more concerned when they find she has invited him for a supposedly secret weekend *à deux* in the country. To save her from herself, they follow her and are as surprised as she is to find that Jerry Ross, the glittering star, is in fact a shy, bespectacled youth yearning for a quiet life. Penitent mum goes back to dad, while Jerry finds true love with daughter.
Not published and not available for production.

LOVE AFTER ALL (1959)

Set in Edwardian days, and based on *The Barber of Seville*, this farce tells the classic story of the mean father who wants to marry off his daughter to wealth, and who is foiled by the true-loving suitor who gets past him in a variety of disguises.
Not published and not available for production.

FOLLOW THE LOVER
and
DOUBLE HITCH

Two one-act plays, only ever presented in amateur productions in Scarborough.
Not published and not available for production.

DAD'S TALE (1960)

Written as a Christmas show to combine the companies of the Scarborough Theatre in the Round and the British Dance Drama Theatre, it was also intended to combine the writing talents of Alan Ayckbourn and David Campton. In fact, Campton wrote a synopsis based on *The Borrowers* which Ayckbourn was unable to work to. The basis remained, but the show became 'the story of how my dad turned into a blackbird'.
Not published and not available for production.

STANDING ROOM ONLY (1961)

Described as 'a new traffic-jam comedy', the play envisages a world in the early twenty-first century in which all roads have been totally paralysed for more than twenty years. A London bus driver and his family live in the bus which he was driving down Shaftesbury Avenue when the jam occurred. That was so long ago that his two grown-up daughters have never known any other home, and indeed he has come to think that the bus's destination board announces his name, Hammersmith, with the letters BRDWY after it being his recommendation from London Transport: 'Best Ruddy Driver We've 'ad Yet'. The engine has been replaced by a garden, and the play looks at the family's attempts to cope with, and circumvent, the bureaucracy of movement and population controls which have been thrown up by the immobilisation of all traffic. Originally, the play ended with the traffic starting to roll again, but one of the revised versions, amended for the proposed West End showing which did not transpire, had the vehicles being removed vertically by helicopter cranes.
Not published and not available for production.

XMAS v. MASTERMIND (1962)

A Christmas show for children, described as 'the most disastrous play I've ever done'. Father Christmas, an unpleasant old man, is faced with a strike by his gnomes. The chief gnome is incited to revolution by the Crimson Golliwog and his gang, who aspire to the takeover of Father Christmas.
Not published and not available for production.

MR. WHATNOT (1963)

Mint, a piano-tuner (played mute throughout), is summoned to The Grange in his professional capacity and becomes entangled in the life of the lord of the manor, his plummy family, his chinless prospective son-in-law and a visiting tweedy lady. Cast out once for ogling the daughter of the house and doing battle over the keyboard with her intended, he returns to play tennis, to have tea and – as this transforms into a fantasy re-run of trench warfare – to wheedle his way (by saving her ladyship from the grenades) into a hero's clinch with the daughter. Accepted now as a house-guest, Mint continues to woo the girl through sustained farcical set-pieces; dinner, retirement to bed and, in the climax to the play, a mimed car-chase and dash across the fields to a wedding in church. The wedding is not Mint's, though the girl finally is.
Published in French's Acting Editions (Samuel French).

MEET MY FATHER (1965)
(subsequently re-titled RELATIVELY SPEAKING)

A pair of strange slippers under the bed strongly suggest to Greg that he is not entirely alone in receiving the favours of his girl-friend Ginny. He pursues her secretly to Bucks to request her father's permission to marry her. Unfortunately, he arrives before her, and Philip, to whom he addresses his request, is not Ginny's father at all, but her former boss and lover, whom she is due to visit to sign off their affair. Philip harbours suspicions about the fidelity of his own wife, Sheila, and immediately assumes that it is she whom Greg is seeking to marry. He refuses his consent, but is content for Greg and Sheila to go off and live together. Greg, however, is still talking about Ginny and understandably finds Philip's suggestion a strange paternal attitude. Ginny pitches in and is able to persuade Philip to play the role of Dad; and in that part, he persuades Greg to allow him a last fling with Ginny on a continental holiday. Sheila, however, has the measure of the situation and converts Philip's plot for an extended amorous ding-dong with Ginny on his own, into a honeymoon for Ginny and Greg. She further manipulates the situation to taunt Philip with his own suspicions of her. *Published by Evans Plays.*

THE SPARROW (1967)

Drenched by the storm, Ed, an unassuming bus conductor, arrives back at his chaotic flat with Evie, the mini-skirted, rather plain girl he has met at the dance hall. As they dry out, Ed convinces Evie that the weather and the time of night have somewhat scuppered the chances of getting her home, and she reluctantly agrees to stay the night in Ed's bed – while he bunks down on the settee. Ed's flatmate, Tony, a cold, flash character, has other ideas, however: Evie spends the night in the bath. In Ed's absence next morning, Tony, through a mixture of bullying and flattery, takes on Evie as his secretary in his 'wholesale business' – an arrangement looked on with scepticism by Julia, Tony's estranged wife who wanders in and who is clearly at least as tough as he is; and with incredulity by Ed, who is less than pleased when 'business' gets in the way of his struggling social relationship with Evie. Slowly, Evie learns the truth: Tony has no business and is employed as a car salesman; and Julia left home after an aberrant roll on the bed with Ed, following one of her frequent rows with Tony. Evie is clearly the tool Tony is using to get back at both Julia and Ed. Julia and Tony return to the flat, obviously in harness once again, and begin a mammoth row in the kitchen. Ed and Evie, pawns no more, steal out to the pub, vowing never to marry. *Not published and not available for production.*

HOW THE OTHER HALF LOVES (1969)

When Bob Phillips's liaison with his boss's wife, Fiona Foster, is in danger of being discovered by their respective spouses, each attempts to wriggle out of suspicion by projecting their own infidelity on to a third – totally innocent and socially retarded – couple, William and Mary Featherstone. The respective spouses, Theresa Phillips and Frank Foster, independently determine to try and help the hapless Featherstones in their supposed problem. Inevitably, their benevolent interference in the life of the Featherstones backfires disastrously and leads to a wild-eyed William descending upon the Phillips household bearing a monkey-wrench and seeking revenge upon Bob for his supposed seduction of Mary. In the *dénouement*, the Featherstones are reconciled, Bob and Fiona are reduced to admitting the truth of their liaison with impunity, and Theresa Phillips and Frank Foster, as a result of another set of misunderstandings, find themselves making a telephone assignation with each other without realising who the other is. Much of the farcical comedy of this plot is in its stagescape, a living/dining room which manages simultaneously to be that of the Phillipses and the Fosters, with the two menages co-existing in the same stage space even when the times do not coincide: thus dinner at the Fosters on Thursday is played simultaneously with dinner at the Phillipses on Friday, with constant dovetailing and crosscutting. *Published by Evans Plays.*

ERNIE'S INCREDIBLE ILLUCINATIONS (1969)

Ernie's imaginings have an embarrassing habit of involving those around him. His parents are on the receiving end of a Gestapo house raid (Ernie saves them by machine-gunning the intruders), his auntie knocks out a heavyweight champion, and his father heroically undertakes a difficult mountain rescue in the public library. The doctor, to whom his parents take Ernie to have his illucinations cured, dismisses it all as mass hysteria and finds himself the drum major of a brass band composed of the patients in his waiting room.
A one-act play for children. Published in French's Acting Editions (Samuel French); and by Hutchinson (in Playbill One, ed. Alan Durband).

COUNTDOWN (1969)

A very brief dialogue, originally part of *Mixed Doubles*, 'an entertainment on marriage' by various authors. The desultory post-prandial conversation of a middle-aged couple is counterpointed by the mutual hostility revealed in the silent (but here voiced) thoughts of each.
Published (in Mixed Doubles) *in French's Acting Editions (Samuel French); and by Methuen.*

THE STORY SO FAR (1970)
(subsequently revised (1972) as ME TIMES ME TIMES ME and re-titled (1978) FAMILY CIRCLES)

Polly, Jenny and Deirdre come down to their parents' home for the weekend to help them celebrate their anniversary. Polly and Jenny have their husbands in tow and Deirdre her current man. Looming over the weekend is a persistent rumour that, despite all appearances to the contrary, something is going seriously wrong between Mum and Dad – indeed, that

he is trying to do away with her – and right to the end, there are little pieces of circumstantial evidence which may be interpreted as hinting at the truth of the rumour. The scenes of the play cover the arrival of the girls and their men: preparing to leave for the celebration dinner; returning from the dinner; and the following morning. By a theatrical conceit (for it is not intended naturalistically as a wife-swapping exercise), the author has each girl paired with a different man in each of the first three scenes; and in the final scene, all nine permutations are intermingled, which makes for a hectic *dénouement*. It is difficult to resist Ayckbourn's own assessment of the play when he says 'it is probably not vintage, but it's got a few good laughs in it; the premise of the play being that, depending upon whom you marry, you become slightly different. And it's quite fun to watch.'
Not published and not available for production.

TIME AND TIME AGAIN (1971)

Returning from a family funeral, Graham and Anna Baker, together with Anna's brother Leonard, are joined for tea by Peter, an employee of Graham's, with his delicious fiancée, Joan – at whom Graham makes a lecherous lunge. This pass is observed by Leonard, the family maverick, as he sits outside in the garden, where he normally repairs to quote poetry and discuss life with the garden gnome, and to reflect upon the rituals of football and cricket which are enacted on the recreation ground just beyond the garden. Peter, a sports fanatic, inveigles the reluctant and frankly useless Leonard into these rituals, while Leonard concentrates rather on wooing Joan, at which he is manifestly more adept. By the onset of the football season, Joan is all set to marry Leonard, but he has quite neglected to inform Peter, the lady's hopeless fiancé, that he has been supplanted in her affections. Recalling Graham's earlier advances towards Joan, however, Peter misreads the situation and launches into a violent attack upon Graham. Leonard witnesses this, but is little motivated to intervene as Graham has dismissed him from the family home. Joan decides that Leonard's conduct has little to do with love for her, and walks out; leaving Peter and Leonard to console each other after the match at having 'mislaid the trophy', but also to agree that 'there's more to life than winning trophies'.
Published in French's Acting Editions (Samuel French).

ABSURD PERSON SINGULAR (1972)

Over three consecutive Christmas Eves, three couples come together to celebrate in one another's homes: we view the parties from the kitchens. First, we visit Sidney and Jane. He is an incurably hearty and pushy man who dominates his obsessively houseproud and accident-prone wife, and who is seeking a bank loan, to develop his interests from the general stores which they run. The guests are his bank manager Ronald and his wife Marion, a lady apparently secure in her supercilious patronage; and Geoffrey and Eva, whose marriage is already clearly in trouble because of his womanising. Geoffrey is an architect angling for the job of designing a new shopping complex – a job towards which Ronald might be able to help him. In act two, we move to Geoffrey and Eva's high-rise flat, where Eva is clearly set on suicide. In absolute silence, she makes several attempts at this, while Geoffrey seeks a doctor and the guests busy themselves with domestic chores and repairs all around her. Marion retreats further into drink amidst disasters on all sides. Finally, we move to Ronald and Marion's house another year later. Marion has sunk deeper into alcoholic isolation, and Geoffrey's design for the shopping centre has collapsed: he is now dependent upon Eva to rebuild his career. Meanwhile, Sidney and Jane's property development scheme has come up trumps: Ronald finds he must woo them for their continued business for the bank, and Geoffrey's future as an architect could hang on their patronage. Fortunes are completely reversed from the position in act one. The party games beloved of Sidney, previously disdained by the other couples, are played: Sidney calls the tune.

Published in French's Acting Editions (Samuel French); by Chatto and Windus and by Penguin (in Three Plays*).*

THE NORMAN CONQUESTS (1973)

Three self-contained plays, featuring the same people at the same house over the same weekend. Each play stands as a complete entity and can be performed independently of the other two; although in practice, all three are usually played on consecutive nights, to be seen in any order.

Table Manners covers events around meal times in the dining room; *Living Together* takes place in the living room; and *Round and Round the Garden* takes up the action as it occurs in the garden. Sarah and Reg arrive to relieve Annie, housebound with her and Reg's bedridden mother, for the weekend. Sarah, whose obsession with order and propriety borders on – and at times tips over into – the hysterical, quickly discovers to her horror that Annie is proposing to spend her weekend away in an East Grinstead hotel with Norman, the assistant librarian husband of her sister Ruth, who believes him to be away at a conference. The idea is quickly squashed with Sarah's intervention, as she tries both to send Norman back home to his wife, and to turn Annie instead towards Tom, the dim local vet, who is a regular visitor to the house but who has never initiated any amorous approach towards her. Norman declines to go home and self-pitifully gets drunk instead. When Ruth is summoned to take charge of her husband, the explosive tensions within the family are released and drag in the hapless Tom, who manages to grasp the wrong end of every proffered stick. Norman bounces from one woman to another, claiming in each case that his only desire is to make them happy. Finally, all three women turn their backs on Norman.

Published in French's Acting Editions (Samuel French); and by Chatto and Windus and Penguin.

ABSENT FRIENDS (1974)

Colin's fiancée has recently drowned and Diana, wife of one of his former friends, Paul, has organised a tea party. The object is that they, along with John and Gordon – also old friends of his – should be re-united in an attempt to help Colin to forget his grief. Gordon can't make it, since, as is his wont, he is ill in bed; but his wife Marge turns up. Both Paul and John (whose bored wife Evelyn turns out to have been briefly laid in the back of a car by Paul – an incident over which John bites his lip, being dependent on Paul for business) are less than enthusiastic. Diana, meanwhile, is profoundly unhappy in her marriage with Paul and suspects him of having a *grande affaire* with Evelyn; while Marge is constantly on the phone to Gordon, who has disaster after disaster through being left on his own in his illness. When Colin arrives, their attempts to take his mind off his tragedy are aborted by his determination to talk of his lost love, and by his wrong-headed attempts to sort out their problems. He is in fact blissfully happy in his sentimental memories, while they suffer the effects of love grown cold.
Published in French's Acting Editions (Samuel French); and by Chatto and Windus and Penguin (in Three Plays*).*

CONFUSIONS (1974)

Five interlinked one-act plays. *Mother Figure*: prompted by a telephone call from their next door neighbour Harry, who is away from home in a hotel in Middlesbrough, Rosemary and Terry pop round to see if his wife and kids are all right. Lucy's life is totally absorbed in her children, and Rosemary and Terry find themselves treated, and spoken to, as children by her. Under this influence, they begin to behave as children, too. Meanwhile, husband Harry turns up in *Drinking Companion* in a hotel bar, where he tries to lure two salesgirls into his bedroom, but succeeds only in getting himself drunk. *Between Mouthfuls* shows two couples, the Pearces and Polly and Martin, at dinner separately in the same restaurant. Martin works for Mr. Pearce, who has just returned from three illicit weeks in Rome with Polly. Mrs. Pearce, discovering this, is furious at her husband's deception and storms out. Polly is furious that, when she tells Martin, his only concern is that it will ruin his promotion prospects: she too storms out. Pearce and Martin retire to the bar for a brandy, in animated conversation. Gordon Gosforth, village publican, has secured the services of his local councillor, Mrs. Pearce, to open the village fete he has supposedly organised, in *Gosforth's Fete*. Sadly, it is hopelessly disorganised. The ailing P.A. system returns to life at the wrong moment to broadcast to the assembled multitude the village teacher's announcement to Gordon that she is pregnant by him – and this drives her cubmaster fiancé to drink. Other disasters include a jammed tea urn which causes the amplifier to blow up, electrocuting Mrs. Pearce; and scaffolding which collapses under the weight of rampaging cub scouts. Finally,

A Talk in the Park is a round of monologues by five characters on park benches, each trying to make contact with the next, while ignoring the plight of the last.
Published in French's Acting Editions (Samuel French).

SERVICE NOT INCLUDED (1974)

Ayckbourn's only television play transmitted as part of BBC2's *Masquerade* series.
At the fancy dress dance to mark the ending of a company conference, the camera follows Jace, the bar waiter, as he serves the delegates and their wives. As he moves from group to group, the desperate undertow of the social occasion – including adultery, alcoholism, boot-licking ambition and the remote and cavalier insensitivity of management – is revealed to him bit by bit, while he remains professionally impervious to it all.
Not published.

JEEVES (1975)

Adaptation of the P.G. Wodehouse stories with book and lyrics by Ayckbourn and score by Andrew Lloyd Webber.
Not published. Original cast recording issued by MCA (MCF 2726).

BEDROOM FARCE (1975)

Ernest and Delia go out to celebrate their anniversary, while their intensely incoherent son Trevor and his neurotic wife Susannah (who are immersed in severe compatibility problems) attend a house-warming party at Malcolm and Kate's. The party is also attended by Jan, who once came close to marrying Trevor, and whose husband Nick is prevented from attending with her by a bad back which confines him to bed. The play is constantly cross-cut among the bedrooms of Ernest and Delia, Malcolm and Kate and Nick and Jan, as they are invaded during the course of a long night by Trevor and Susannah and their marital mess. In the process, the relationships between the natural inhabitants of the three bedrooms are inevitably stretched and infected.
Published in French's Acting Editions (Samuel French); and by Chatto and Windus and Penguin (in Three Plays*).*

JUST BETWEEN OURSELVES (1976)

Dennis is a hearty blusterer, immersed in chaotic do-it-yourselfery in his garage and wholly insensitive to the needs of his wife Vera, whose personality is being systematically undermined in their home by the poisonous influence of his mother, who lives with them. Into this situation walks the feeble, mildly hypochondriac Neil, seeking to buy Dennis's old Morris Minor as a birthday present for his wife, Pam. It is clear, however, that Pam's needs are more basic and that she regards the car, which declines to work anyway, as a poor substitute.

As we meet the characters on three separate birthdays during the course of a year, Pam becomes increasingly sour in her relationship with Neil, who leans on Dennis for support and is given ill-informed and disastrous investment advice as a result. Vera is finally driven into catatonia, but even this fails to shake Dennis into the vaguest awareness of the responsibility he has for her condition.

Published in French's Acting Editions (Samuel French); and by Chatto and Windus (in Joking Apart and Other Plays*).*

TEN TIMES TABLE (1977)

Using the local hotel ballroom as a committee room, a group of socially more-or-less dispossessed members of the community are brought together by Ray, a local shopkeeper, and his wife Helen (apparently as an extension to her activities with the Tory Ladies), to organise a town pageant. The would-be actors include a couple whose marriage is in the process of breaking up; a bureaucratically sound but otherwise ineffective local councillor, saddled with an ancient and deaf mother constantly in need of tasks to keep her occupied; a Marxist schoolteacher, with one common-law wife in tow, and seeking both a platform for his views and more female adulation (which he gets from a lady dog-breeder). The subject for the pageant is to be a hitherto unknown episode in the town's history, when the Earl of Dorset led the militia into the square to trounce a bunch of rebellious workers: the Massacre of the Pendon Twelve. The ideological polarities of the original event are rapidly adopted by different factions on the committee; and as the leftist faction increasingly comes to refer to the pageant as a rally, the lady dog-breeder's gun-toting fascist brother is recruited to mastermind the right-wing response, and, as it transpires, to provoke a bloody confrontation all decked out in motley. With the pageant farcically over, the committee becomes once again the bunch of individuals it originally was, their personal problems still intact.

Published in French's Acting Editons (Samuel French); and by Chatto and Windus (in Joking Apart and Other Plays*).*

JOKING APART (1978)

The old vicarage is occupied by Richard and Anthea, an unmarried couple with her children by her earlier marriage. Meanwhile, the vicar and his wife, Hugh and Louise, live with their son in a small cottage at the bottom of the garden. Richard is a partner in business with Sven, an infinitely pedantic and preening work-fanatic, whose apparently boundless self-respect, fed by his doting wife Olive, is largely based in the fact that he was once Finnish junior tennis champion. They employ Brian, who innocently gave Anthea and her children sanctuary when her marriage broke up and who has nursed an obsessive passion for her ever since. This he unenthusiastically attempts to sublimate in a constant stream of inappropriate girl-friends. Over a twelve-year span, these people meet for social occasions in the garden of

Richard and Anthea – an easy-going, endlessly generous, sensitive and successful couple, to whom everything comes easily, and who seek to give of their good fortune to the others through their hospitality. Louise is unable from the outset to manage her son, and his refusal to have any communication with his parents, combines with the loss of her husband's love (Hugh conceives and declares a ludicrous passion for Anthea), to drive her into manic depression and drugged retreat. The fiercely competitive Sven is made increasingly aware that he is losing ground in business to Richard, despite his obsessive hard work (contrasted with Richard's casual flair); and even at tennis, his narrow victory over Richard is revealed to be only because Richard played left-handed ('I thought he needed to win', says Richard). Sven suffers a heart attack and descends into profound bitterness at the injustice of life. Debbie, Anthea's daughter, declines, as she comes of age, to continue the family's style of patronage by refusing to become another in Brian's list of Anthea-substitutes.

Published in French's Acting Editions (Samuel French); and by Chatto and Windus (in Joking Apart and Other Plays*).*

MEN ON WOMEN ON MEN (1978)

A late-night revue. In sketch and song (the music is by Paul Todd), the revue worries, with little mercy or optimism, but with perception, poignancy and wit, at a variety of facets of the relationship between men and women, and at the self-deceit in their perceptions of each other and themselves.

Not published. Live performance recording issued on cassette TSJTITR 001 by the Stephen Joseph Theatre in the Round, Scarborough.

SISTERLY FEELINGS (1979)

What the audience sees may be any one of four possible versions of *Sisterly Feelings*, depending upon the toss of a coin at the end of the first scene and the decision of one of two actresses at the end of the second scene. Scenes One and Four remain constant, but there are two versions each of Scenes Two and Three. Following the funeral of his wife, Ralph brings his family to a favourite spot on Pendon Common. With him are his two daughters, Abigail and Dorcas – trailing businessman husband Patrick and radical poet boyfriend Stafford respectively; his student son Melvyn – with his fiancée Brenda and her brother Simon; and his brother-in-law, Detective Inspector Len, with his wife Rita. Both Abigail and Dorcas are attracted to the bronzed and athletic Simon. When Patrick has to leave prematurely to attend a business meeting, the rest are left with insufficient cars to get them all home. Either Abigail or Dorcas will have to walk home with Simon. They toss a coin and the loser goes home by car. Scene Two is a picnic four months later. Responsible for the arrangements of the picnic is whichever daughter lost the toss in Scene One. The other daughter arrives at the picnic by bicycle, accompanied by Simon, and the proceedings are disturbed by the unexpected presence at the picnic of the husband/boyfriend whom Simon is currently displacing. The picnic is curtailed by a rainstorm, at which point the daughter accompanying Simon has to decide whether to remain with him – and face a soaking bike ride – or to return to her original partner. On her decision rests the choice of a third scene: either a proposed romantic night under canvas with Simon and Abigail (which goes badly awry, thanks to vigilante patrolling by policeman Len), or the annual cross-country derby (which equally goes badly awry), in which Simon challenges the police champion. Meanwhile, Melvyn has failed his exams to become a doctor and has made Brenda pregnant. By the beginning of Scene Four, depending on which version of the work has been played, Simon has enjoyed the favours of either Abigail or Dorcas, or of both in either order. Scene Four follows Melvyn's wedding to Brenda, as the family again gathers on the common to humour Ralph, who came here with his bride on his wedding day. Abigail and Dorcas are back with the partners they started with in Scene One, aware, perhaps of the arbitrariness of the decisions they have taken to change the course of their lives. Simon is an embarrassed best man.

Published in French's Acting Editions (Samuel French); and by Chatto and Windus.

TAKING STEPS (1979)

As in *How the Other Half Loves*, the set is a leading character in this farce. Here, the attic, master bedroom and living room of The Pines, along with two staircases, are flattened into a single stage space, and action is frequently concurrent in all parts of the house. Elizabeth, a pop dancer, is about to leave her bucket manufacturer husband Roland, after three and a half months of marriage. She has summoned her brother Mark to comfort Roland when, on his return from work, he will read her farewell note. Mark, however, has other preoccupations: his fiancée Kitty abandoned him at the altar to run off with a waiter, and she is just now being returned to him by the police after being picked up on suspicion of soliciting on Haverstock Hill. While Mark takes Elizabeth to the station, and establishes the depressed Kitty in the spare bed in the attic, Tristram Watson, the befuddled junior partner of Roland's solicitor, arrives to complete the documentation for the sale of The Pines to Roland by Bainbridge, a local builder, whom Roland also wishes to retain to do repairs and alterations to the building – which in earlier days was a high class brothel, and which is rumoured to be haunted still by one of the whores who formerly inhabited it. She, the story goes, seduces current occupants during the night and kills them at daybreak. On reading Elizabeth's note, Roland, believing himself alone in the house with Watson and Bainbridge – and already much the worse for drink – breaks down and prevails upon Watson to stay the night at the house to keep him company, postponing all talk of completion to the morrow. Unable to face sleeping in the master bedroom, he instals Watson in there, while he retires to the spare bed in the attic. Hearing him approach, Kitty abandons the suicide note she had been writing and hides in a cupboard – where she becomes trapped as Roland

shifts the bed across the door. Meanwhile, Elizabeth has had a change of heart and returns in the dark, crawling into bed with Watson and proceeding to pleasure him in the belief that he is Roland. Ever susceptible, Watson accepts the advances as those of the putative ghostly whore. So ends Act One. Act Two plays out the farcical logic of this situation, with Mark discovering Kitty's suicide note, which they assume to have been written by Roland. Confusion piles upon confusion, Watson and Kitty discover each other (and leave), and Elizabeth decides once more to leave Roland – or does she?
Published in French's Acting Editions (Samuel French); and by Chatto and Windus.

SUBURBAN STRAINS (1980)

Ayckbourn's collaborator in this musical play was composer Paul Todd. Caroline, a teacher, throws out her layabout actor husband, after finding him in bed with one of her pupils, and takes as lover a doctor, whose main concern appears to be to demolish her and reconstruct her to his own prescription. Her two relationships are presented in filmic counterpoint, while parents, professional colleagues and even her lover's wife observe from the periphery, offering advice and sermons. She ends up back with husband Kevin, now without illusions, as together they proclaim: 'Why not settle for today, and cuddle up tonight?'

FIRST COURSE (1980)

A lunch-time musical revue, written in collaboration with Paul Todd: ten songs charting impressions of the decades from 1890 to the 1980s.

SECOND HELPING (1980)

A lunch-time musical revue, written in collaboration with Paul Todd: ten songs about aspects of love.

SEASON'S GREETINGS (1980)

Belinda and Neville have gathered family and friends around them for a traditional family Christmas. Amongst them are Harvey, a retired security guard, who, when not immersed in old films on television, sees himself as a one-man vigilante patrol defending Civilised Standards; Belinda's 38-year-old unmarried sister, Rachel, who has invited along a writer friend, Clive; and Neville's brother-in-law, Bernard, a failed doctor whose ritual Christmas puppet show annually bores the children as much as it fills the adults with foreboding. Harvey immediately takes a dislike to Clive and proceeds to build fantasies about him as a homosexual looter. Clive and Belinda, however, fall for each other in a big way and disastrously attempt midnight consummation beneath the Christmas tree, following a declaration by Rachel that she is not really interested in sex and that what she wants from

Clive is friendship. It is convenient, on Boxing Day, to pass off the previous night's *fracas* as a drunken romp; but Clive knows it wasn't and, to save further embarrassment, arranges to leave by the first train the following morning. He duly leaves – though not by train – after Harvey's hate-fantasy goes horribly over the top, and Bernard tragically confirms his medical incompetence.

PHOTOGRAPH CREDITS

For permission to reproduce the photographs that appear in this book, acknowledgement is made to the following: Ken Boden: pages 49, 53, 62, 78, 93; Marija Braut: page 121; Nobby Clark: page 150; Anthony Crickmay: page 161; Ernst Hausknost: page 118 (bottom); John Haynes: page 89; Angus McBean: page 77; Richard S. Morse: page 82; Rigmov Mydtskov and Steen Rønne: page 118 (top); Houston Rogers: pages 69, 75; Alec Russell: pages 123, 133, 142, 171; Scarborough Evening News: page 138; Thames Television: page 115; Trygve Schønfelder: page 166; Rafel Sedláček: page 127 (bottom); Sam Siegel: page 91; Jutta Ungelenk-Stamp: page 117; Victoria Theatre, Stoke-on-Trent: pages 59, 64, 65. The posters on pages 102 and 154 were designed by the Drawing Room, Warwick.